LEGITIMATING
THE
CHINESE
ECONOMIC
REFORMS

SUNY SERIES IN SPEECH COMMUNICATION
DUDLEY D. CAHN JR., EDITOR

Cover calligraphy by Zhang Pengfei

Published by
State University of New York Press, Albany

For information, address State University of New York
Press, State University Plaza, Albany, N.Y. 12246

Production by E. Moore
Marketing by Fran Keneston

Library of Congress Cataloging-in-Publication Data

Kluver, Alan R., 1964-
    Legitimating the Chinese economic reforms : a rhetoric of myth and
orthodoxy / Alan R. Kluver.
       p.   cm. — (SUNY series in speech communication)
    Includes bibliographical references and index.
    ISBN 0-7914-2991-1 (hardcover : alk. paper). — ISBN 0-7914-2992-X
(pbk. : alk. paper)
    1. China—Economic policy—1976- 2. China—Economic
conditions—1976- 3. Mixed economy—China. 4. Socialism—China.
5. Legitimacy of governments—China. I. Title. II. Series.
HC427.92.K58 1996
338.951—dc20
                                                                        95-36331
                                                                            CIP

10 9 8 7 6 5 4 3 2 1

LEGITIMATING THE CHINESE ECONOMIC REFORMS

A Rhetoric of Myth and Orthodoxy

ALAN R. KLUVER

State University of New York Press

Contents

Preface

This study grew out of a chance gift from the Foreign Affairs Bureau at Jiangxi Normal University, Nanchang, Jiangxi, People's Republic of China, in 1987. The Bureau graciously provided me a copy of the Party Documents from the Thirteenth Congress of the Chinese Communist Party in that year. As I studied the documents, I became fascinated with the rhetorical processes involved in Chinese politics.

As China's reform policies have continued, and the national politics have continued to be turbulent, China has become increasingly open to outside observation and analysis. It is hoped that this will be a small contribution to a growing trend to analyze China from outside of the disciplinary frameworks that have historically supported China studies. It is also my hope that this will contribute to a trend to approach rhetorical studies from non-Western perspectives, that the discipline of rhetoric might gain from a broader cultural understanding.

This book is the result of several years of contributions by outstanding scholars. Foremost among them are Tom Hollihan, Walter Fisher, and Stanley Rosen. I wish to thank each of them for their insight, direction, and friendship. Professors Hollihan and Fisher contributed great insight into the rhetorical dimensions of this work, as well as close and careful editing. Professor Rosen enthusiastically supported my efforts to bring a rhetorical perspective to bear on Chinese politics, and often reminded me that in China, things are not always as they seem.

I also must acknowledge the contributions from Chinese students and scholars in the United States, in both Southern California and Oklahoma. Bai Chunsheng, Deng Zhenghan, Wang Yiping, Lou Wei, Xu Xiangming, and Xu Junyi were foremost among many others who gave me tremendous encouragement and support in completing this work.

Pam Kluver has contributed greatly to the completion of this book. To her I owe a profound debt for her devotion, encouragement, support, and love.

I would also like to acknowledge my mother and father, Mary and Ordell Kluver, for first opening my eyes to Asia, and demonstrating what a heart of love and a commitment to the welfare of others can accomplish.

All of these people have made invaluable contributions to this book. Needless to say, all the errors are mine alone.

Finally, I would like to acknowledge the following for permission to reprint from their publications:

Princeton University Press, for permission to quote from Han Minzhu, ed., *Cries for Democracy: Writings and Speeches from the 1989 Chinese Democracy Movement* (1990).

Cambridge University Press, for permission to quote from Steven Sangren, "History and the Rhetoric of Legitimacy: The Ma Tsu Cult of Taiwan," in *Comparative Studies in Society and History*, vol. 30 (1988).

Journal of Asian History, for permission to quote from Lance Eccles, "The Seizure of the Mandate: Establishment of the Legitimacy of the Liang Dynasty," vol. 23, no. 2, 1989, pp. 169–180.

China Quarterly, for permission to reprint from Stuart Schram, "'Economics in Command?' Ideology and Policy since the Third Plenum," vol. 99, 1984, pp. 417–461.

Foreign Language Press, Beijing, for permission to quote from *The Twelfth National Congress of the CPC (September, 1982; Documents of the Thirteenth National Congress of the Communist Party of China (1987); Documents of the Fourteenth National Congress of the Communist Party of China (1992); Resolution on Chinese History (1949–81);* and "Communique of the Third Plenary Session of the Eleventh Central Committee of the Communist Party of China," published in *Peking Review*, no. 52, December 29, 1978.

1 The Rhetorical Construction of Chinese Political Reality

China's radical economic reform program, often referred to as "China's Second Revolution," has, by the mid-1990s, become fully entrenched into Chinese society. Stock markets, entrepreneurship, and private enterprise have been reintroduced with a vengeance, after nearly half a century of absence. These economic transformations have so reinvigorated the national economy that they have raised fears among some of the rise of regional conflict. Perhaps more important to social and cultural scholars, however, is that the reforms have raised difficult and unsettling questions as to the legacy of the Communist movement, especially the Maoist past.

With the dissolution of the former Soviet bloc, the world has witnessed the breathtaking speed at which nations can fundamentally alter the economic and ideological frameworks upon which their political systems exist, and so in contrast the reform movement itself is not particularly remarkable. What makes the Chinese reform movement noteworthy is that market-oriented reforms have been introduced in a society that still loudly proclaims its allegiance to Marxism, albeit Marxism with Chinese characteristics. While Russia has recanted from Marxism–Leninism and is actively seeking to build a capitalistic society, China retains its allegiance to the socialist principles on which it is founded, with the ultimate goal of achieving the perfect Communist state.

Although the reform program provides fertile ground for analysis from many fields, including political science, economics, and history; one of the more neglected aspects is the radical change in the way the Chinese think about the reform program. The individual components of the reform agenda, including private enterprise, stock markets, and the rise of entrepreneurship, had all been repudiated in previous decades as not only illegal and immoral, but also as anachronistic. How could it be that all of these are now accepted as not only benign, but also necessary? The early legitimacy of the Communist Party and the Communist revolution itself rested in large part on an explicit belief that China's future lie in communism. Both China's declared identity and orthodoxy stood in stark contrast to the freewheeling nature of the reforms. The question, simply stated, is thus: How does one introduce a stock market and call it Marxism?

This question is more than academic, but of immense importance for all who seek to understand recent Chinese history, and indeed, social change in general. Observers of China during the 1989 Tiananmen Square movement were puzzled by the question of why such popular protests could arise during the period of greatest economic growth and increasing riches. In many ways, this paradox undercuts many of our favorite theories for explaining social change. If we see social change as resulting from economic dissatisfaction, in particular, then we are left at a loss to explain the tremendous upheaval during the Tiananmen demonstrations, when the entire society was benefiting from increasing economic opportunities. Moreover, if social change is conceived as resulting from social and political stagnation, inhibiting creativity, then we are left with no explanation of the demonstrations, arising as they did at a time of unprecedented individual freedom and opportunity in China.

Perhaps it is better to conceive of social change as arising from the mythical and ideological dimensions that lie at the heart of national identity. When we analyze it in this way, the introduction of the reform program has clearly introduced a legitimation crisis of epic proportions into contemporary Chinese politics, at both an ideological and institutional level. Ideologically, the nature of the reforms strikes at the heart of traditional Marxism, which posits the evolutionary disappearance of private property. Many of the reforms are not only capitalistic, but are directly contradictory to the policies of Mao Zedong, on whom the entire Chinese political structure rested for decades. The legitimation struggles of the Western world seem to pale in comparison to the drastic implications of such a clear reversal of what was once clearly taught as China's destiny and glory. As one analyst has remarked, the reforms mean nothing less than "the decline of Communism in China."[1]

This ideological crisis takes on its epic dimensions because of the great importance of ideology in Chinese political life. As I will demonstrate in Chapter 2, Chinese political and social life for centuries has relied on ideology for stability. Whereas specific political structures might rise and fall, a common ideological system has been a paramount concern for Chinese rulers. The undoing of what was considered a stable ideological anchor threatens to undo the entirety of Chinese politics and society.

This crisis has significant ideological dimensions, but also profound institutional implications. Economist Peter Lichtenstein argues that economic reform involves a tremendous upheaval of social stability, amounting to "the destruction, the creation, and the preservation of institutions."[2] The legitimacy of the Chinese Communist Party, for example, rests on a certain vision of China's past and future, a vision that has been largely dismantled by the processes of reform. Deng Xiaoping and others, though, have attempted to maintain the primacy of the CCP while instituting a whole new way of life, complete with a different ideological anchor for society. Many of the institutions that have governed Chinese life for decades have become increasingly irrelevant and anachronistic.

This legitimation crisis is the reason for the explosion of political activity throughout China during the spring and summer of 1989. For a brief moment, the citizens and leaders of China were faced with the clear ideological and institutional tensions introduced by the reforms. The Tiananmen movement exposed the tensions, but did not resolve them. The resolution of those tensions must be a rhetorical resolution, and any rhetorical resolution will be years in the making. Moreover, this legitimation crisis is the direct concern of this book, and remains one of the foremost problems facing China's current and future leadership. How can one of the world's largest economies completely reverse itself, while remaining under the control of the very Party that had for decades pursued the opposite course?

The crisis surrounding the economic reforms differs from crises in the West not only in its proportion, but also in its resolution. Specifically, I argue that the political discourse legitimating the reforms serves a different function than similar discourse in Western nations. Political discourse in the People's Republic works in a trickle-down fashion, in that it is carefully designed by the leadership to have the greatest possible persuasive impact on the populace. Western political discourse, especially in recent years, has been designed not to persuade the populace, but to appease them. Whereas Western discourse is contractual, with little theoretical dimensions, Chinese discourse is eminently ideological and theoretical, and carefully designed so as to seem unchanging and universal.

The implications of this study for understanding issues surrounding legitimation are numerous. We will attempt to address these more fully in Chapter 2, but here we will briefly comment that this study illustrates a legitimation crisis caused to a large extent by the government's own policies and actions. In other words, it is the Chinese government and the Chinese Communist Party (CCP) in particular that has begun the process of its own unraveling. This raises an important question: How can a government respond to external necessities while maintaining an internally consistent ideology in a nation that prizes ideological stability? A second important issue is this: Can a political party or institution renegotiate its political legitimacy? In large part, this is what the CCP has attempted; to renegotiate the basis of its legitimacy, from a Party designed to protect peasants from the rich, and in fact, to eliminate the rich, to a party designed to make sure everybody gets rich. We will explore the ideological difficulties inherent in this transformation and develop some conclusions that we can make regarding the rhetoric of legitimation.

I will attempt to analyze this fundamental crisis as well as its tentative resolution through a rhetorical analysis of the discourses generated by the Party congresses since the onset of the reform movement. We are reminded by Yan Jiaqi, an influential Chinese dissident and political theorist, that "the rules and methods by which men gain power are of extreme significance in human affairs."[3] Significant, indeed, since the increasing power of the State due to technological and organizational advances means that these rules and methods are used to legitimate social, economic, and political systems that dominate human life to an extent unimaginable in previous generations. Moreover, the rules and methods by which rulers gain power are increasingly seen as not merely organizational and political, but rhetorical. By turning our attention exclusively to the rhetorical reconstruction of the dominant political ideology, we can see clearly the "ways and methods" by which an entire national mindset has been refashioned. It is to our own peril that we ignore the rhetorical means of power.

I seek in this volume to contribute to the small but growing cadre of works that attempt to understand Chinese culture, society, and politics from within a paradigm of communication. I argue that culture and all its attendant systems are functions of and embedded within human symbolic activity.[4] Politics, in this view, is not so much due to the manipulation of raw military or economic power or sociological factors as much as it is due to the symbolic constructions that surround it.

One of the earliest scholars to view Chinese political life from this perspective was Godwin Chu. Chu envisioned communication as an active force in social and structural change and established the role of communication in establishing the reality of political and social life:

> Communication is not . . . merely . . . a stimulus or . . . a change agent that brings about effects in terms of specific individual response. Rather, communication is . . . the basic social process, encompassing an intricate entirety of verbal stimulus and response.[5]

Further, an understanding of communicative practices is vital for understanding political socialization and China's political culture. Chu argued that Chinese political communication differs from Western political discourse in that it is explicitly normative and value-oriented, oriented toward changing the values of the audience. The Chinese government, according to Chu, views channels of communication primarily as a means of explicitly shaping political consciousness, rather than as a means for disseminating information. If this is so, we gain some initial clues for understanding the role of political discourse in resolving rhetorical tensions. Primarily, we see that political discourse functions to teach, and in one sense, to bind China's populace to a certain ideology.

I seek to go beyond Chu's initial steps in that Chu does not focus on what has been traditionally identified as *rhetoric*. Rather, he sees interpersonal and small group communication as the most dynamic element of political socialization in China. Policy documents and proclamations from Beijing, in Chu's view, serve a secondary role in providing a context for interpersonal pressure and commitments. Purposeful communication from the elites to the populace serves only as a tool for the more important business of interpersonal persuasion.

In contrast, I argue that the legitimation of the reforms rests on the ability of the Party to create a compelling narrative that mandates the reforms, an argument consistent both with recent Chinese history and with the ideological constraints that exist within the nation. Harry Harding asserts that "the reforms have been the result of extraordinary political engineering by a coalition of reform-minded leaders led by Deng Xiaoping."[6] This political engineering involves an intensive *rhetorical* battle to change the Chinese national identity and to define the ruling ideology, a battle that has been carried out in newspapers, editorials, books, proclamations, speeches, and Party meetings.

It is clear that the role of communication in governmental legitimation is vital in that social reality is established through symbolic means. In an insightful analysis of the role of communication in defining Chinese public consciousness, Michael Schoenhals argues that the role of formalized power language is often ignored by Western scholars, at their own peril. In particular, Schoenhals argues that linguistic (rhetorical) formulations, well familiar to all who study China, lie at the heart of the national political process.[7]

Schoenhals argues that political language is formalized language, and that power relationships are embedded in the ways in which political formulations are phrased. Although the Chinese government controls the media and other outlets of expression, by far the most controlling aspect of political thought lies not in institutions such as the official press, but rather in the formalized use of language. The strict linguistic formulations that emerge from Chinese politics, formulations such as "Long live Chairman Mao," "The Four Modernizations," "Oppose Spiritual Pollution," and "Socialism with Chinese Characteristics," serve to circumscribe the reality that can be described, and policies are launched or scuttled in large part by the ways in which they can be expressed. Schoenhals argues that:

> The subject of the use and abuse of formulations is subject to constant strategic deliberation at the highest levels of the CCP. In some cases the process of policy making is indistinguishable from the process of policy formulation. Policy implementation at all levels is affected by concerns with questions like

How should this be put? What happens if we put it with that? Will putting it like this put people off? What do they mean by putting it differently? Can we really let them put it like that?[8]

These questions illustrate the intense rhetorical analysis to which policies are exposed before they are made public. Although all political systems rely on careful formulation of political language, the Chinese case is unique because of the ways in which the use of the language lends itself to easy, rigid formulations, formulations that in turn mandate and proscribe political theory. In the view of the CCP, inappropriate formulations lead to "ideological confusion," and thus inappropriate behavior. For example, in the late 1970s, party theorists declared that there was no reality behind the slogan "capitalist-roader," and thus the slogan was declared unscientific and therefore prohibited. To allow the slogan to continue to have currency would have implied that the theoretical foundation for the slogan had validity, a theoretical implication that would have denied Deng Xiaoping political legitimacy.

Chinese propagandists are acutely aware of the persuasive and emotional impact of wordplay, and dub those most powerful formulations as "scientific." The phrase might have either one clear meaning, or a multitude of meanings, providing for a variety of subtle changes. In order to meet the needs Party propagandists, periodically updated annotated lists of scientific formulations are maintained by agencies such as the People's Liberation Army. In this scheme, some ideas are never able to enter the public consciousness, since there are no politically acceptable words to convey them:

The use of 'incorrect,' 'inappropriate,' and 'unscientific' formulations is not condoned, and those who insist upon using such formulations will be denied access to wider audiences. Only by replicating or mimicking the formal qualities of the discourse of the state can critics of the state make their voices heard . . . the CCP achieves far more with far less by manipulating the form rather than the content of the discourse.[9]

In scientific formulations, form and content are one. If every reference must be to what *is*, no reference can be made to what *could be*. China's leaders have been intimately involved in the prescription of form and have felt free to label formalistic elements of all forms of literature and art as either "revolutionary" or "counterrevolutionary." For example, after the Revolution of 1949, Mao Zedong himself attacked the use of the traditional "eight-legged essay" as antirevolutionary.[10] Only a few top leaders have the right to introduce new formulations without approval from an even higher leader. Thus, the government controls the introduction of new ideas. By controlling the form, the leadership controls ideological innovation itself.

Chinese politics, then, rests on a "language game" that must be recognized to understand political change and stasis.[11] Kenneth Burke clearly articulated the view that all human activity is constituted and constrained by language. Language use is inherently rhetorical, in that rhetoric is "rooted in an essential function of language itself, . . . the use of language as a symbolic means of inducing cooperation in beings that by nature respond to symbols."[12]

The process of naming, or identifying, a situation, is crucial in the later development of any human action. In naming a situation, reality is defined for those who take part in the language, and a motive for dealing with the situation is proposed. Political discourse is itself a form of "secular prayer," in that it serves a corrective function; making drastic policies seem wholly acceptable, and inconsequential policies seem wholly radical. All political documents are substantive, in that they create a world, and, as such, a set of motives.[13] In other words, constitutions really do *constitute* reality, since the language we use to describe a reality becomes that very reality. Murray Edelman carries this one step further when he argues that a political constitution, a linguistic construction, "legitimizes in morally unquestionable postulates the predatory use of such bargaining weapons as groups possess . . . [and] fixes as socially unquestionable fact the primacy of law and of a social order."[14] The language of a constitution (or any other political touchstone) establishes as inevitable, and morally unquestionable, the power relationships within a society.

Language defines not only political life, but also economics. Donald McCloskey argues that the field of economics, as well as any other human symbolic endeavor, is fruitfully understood under the rubric of rhetoric, or the study of how people persuade.[15] For the economic reforms to be implemented and maintained, radical changes had to occur in the *discourse* of the nation. A new image of China had to be rhetorically imprinted into the national consciousness, and the ruling orthodoxy had to be altered so as to allow the radical economic changes. This rhetorical process has altered the structural and economic relationships and values upon which "New China" has been based.

If we are correct in assuming that language constrains social and political life to this extent (and I think we are), then the subtle transformation of China's constitution and dominant rhetorical artifacts (in the documents of the Party congresses) demolished and replaced the existing order of values and relationships. In establishing a new set of economic policies and regulations, the rhetoric of the reform movement encourages a new national identity, a new governing ideology, and a new imperial order, one every bit as powerful, if not more so, than the system of control inherited from the Emperors.

With this perspective in mind, then, the economic reforms taking place under Deng's sponsorship lose the sense of inevitability that often characterizes their discussion. Rather, we recognize that the reforms are taking place against a background of internal debate within the nation as to the proper ideological basis for modernization. As the very basis for the reforms relies on the rhetorical construction of a sound ideological basis, understanding the rhetoric of the reform movement is the proper place from which to begin any further analysis of China's economic and political life.

In order to illustrate the rhetorical campaign to legitimate the reforms, I will focus on the documents arising from the Party congresses held since the death of Mao Zedong. The addresses from these congresses are considered to be key predictors of future governmental policy. Although the reforms have been introduced, nurtured, and in large part legitimated through other forms of communication, particularly the mass media, it is the Party congresses that not only set the immediate political agendas, but serve a symbolic role in establishing the legitimacy of policy. Whereas newpaper editorials and articles in journals reflect ideological battles, the Party congresses reveal the winners. In addition, a new Central Committee is typically chosen at these meetings, to serve until the next scheduled Congress, and revisions are made to the national Constitution. As the Central Committee is the ruling group of the nation, the makeup of its membership is important for the direction of the nation. The particular outcome of Party congresses is always determined during work conferences held beforehand, and the actual Congress serves to disseminate the wishes and perspectives of the top leadership.

The formal or keynote address from each Party Congress is often delivered by one of the top leaders of the Party, normally the secretary general, and serves as the centerpiece of the Congress documents. As the Congress is taken to be the key statement of the nation's goals and priorities for the next several years, in mandatory small group political meetings, each of these speeches becomes the center of attention for study and application.

We should note that because of the role of the Party leadership in predetermining the outcome of these congresses, the speeches of individual leaders do not necessarily serve as reliable indicators of that individual's thought. Instead, the speeches most often reflect the current consensus within the Party hierarchy, since each speech is usually derived from a process of ghostwriting and the input of the Party on all major speeches. Individual speeches, then, reflect the "will of the Party." Each speech is addressed to multiple audiences and reflects the input of a variety of influences, such as competing political factions.[16]

The rhetorical significance of the speeches extends far beyond the immediate setting in which they are delivered. Especially during the mid-1980s, when the status of the reforms was still somewhat uncertain, the entire nation of China was organized into a vast network of small groups that served as channels of communication. These small groups, organized around neighborhoods or work units, would meet regularly (weekly or twice-weekly, normally) and in the group context, discuss the editorials and Party documents sent down from the central leadership. Although both the regularity and the importance of these meetings have decreased, they have served as the contexts in which much of the legitimation rhetoric of the government has been disseminated throughout the society throughout the period of the reforms.

In this study, we will examine four major meetings that have taken place since Mao's death; the Third Plenum of the Eleventh Party Congress (1978) in 1978, the Twelfth Party Congress in 1982, the Thirteenth Party Congress in 1987, and the Fourteenth Party Congress in 1992. These meetings redefined China's leadership and focus, and provided the direction for the coming decades. The speeches to be examined include those of Deng Xiaoping, Hu Yaobang, Zhao Ziyang, and Jiang Zemin, thus representing not only China's key reformers (Deng, Hu, and Zhao), but also Jiang, who has not been a key element in the reform faction, but did replace Zhao as Party secretary after the Tiananmen Square movement of 1989. Through a careful analysis of these documents, it is possible to chart the rhetorical trajectory of the reform program.

Each speech will be analyzed to determine the ways in which the document attempts to accommodate the existing orthodoxy, while ideologically legitimating the reforms. In addition to these speeches, I will examine the 1981 *Resolution on CPC History* in order to illustrate its contribution to the demystification of Mao Zedong and the ideological grounding of Deng Xiaoping's role as the new leader. Each of these documents has served a key role in progressively implementing a new understanding of ideological orthodoxy and the nature of socialism. When their influence is considered collectively, it becomes clear the documents have radically reshaped the Chinese ideological consciousness, and provided the justification for reforms that would have been considered unthinkable at the time of Mao's death.

A brief discussion as to the translation of the relevant documents is in order. It goes without saying that any serious discussion of rhetorical artifacts must be grounded in an understanding of the primary language, rather than in translation. I fully agree with this principle, and in response will make note of any variation between the Chinese formulations and English translations that affect the understanding of the concept. However, given the widespread use and importance of the key concepts that I will examine, it is not necessary constantly to refer to primary language materials. Rather, in order to guarantee the accessibility of my conclusions to a broader audience, I will refer to English language versions of the primary sources.

There are two primary sources of documents for this study; materials published by the Foreign Languages Press in Beijing and translations from the United States Department of State Foreign Broadcast Information Service (FBIS). For the purposes of this study, these two sources will provide adequate translations. I make this judgment based on the following reasons. First, I will be focusing on the official government discourse surrounding the economic reforms. Thus, I am most interested in examining not what was said, but what was *officially* said. It is to be expected that official publications from Beijing have been subjected to intense official scrutiny and revision after the original speech was delivered; however, the principles of translation and editing are the same as those in place for the original release of any document in Chinese. As Lieberthal and Dickson have remarked, "Scholars should not forget that government officials, whether American or Chinese, are doing the selection. . . . What is included or excluded reflects government interests and concerns."[17] In other words, any distortion that occurs in the translation occurs according to the principles geared toward the government's interest. Since it is just as important to find precise foreign translations as it is to come up with precise words for domestic usage, it can be assumed that the translation conveys exactly what China's top leaders want it to convey. In this sense, it is to our advantage to examine documents that have been heavily scrutinized and edited, because my goal is to demonstrate the official explanation for the reforms.

For the sake of convenience, I occasionally refer to FBIS materials rather than official Foreign Language Press documents, since many of the older documents are not readily accessible. I do not believe that this will significantly affect my analysis, in that the Chinese media attempts to adhere to stock formulations and phrases when referring to important policies. Since the FBIS translations are based on official media reports, we can expect there to be little variance from the same general principles stated above. The linguistic formulations and phrases are well known and identified by most analysts, and the FBIS translations can be reasonably trusted to translate documents according to the principles of language precision and specificity. Indeed, it is normally only Taiwanese analysts who choose to use different English translations to refer to certain stock phrases, such as the "primary stage of socialism," which some Taiwanese occasionally translate as the "first stage of socialism."

The organizing principle in this book is chronological, in that I will turn in each chapter to demonstrate how each stage of the reform process is marked by a theoretical emphasis that allows for further latitude in the implementation of reforms. The subsequent chapters will be arranged as follows:

Chapter 2: The Mythical and Ideological Dimensions of Political Legitimacy. This chapter examines the role of rhetoric in establishing political legitimacy, and especially the rhetorical bases of legitimacy in China. I will discuss the role of the Mandate of Heaven and virtue in the classical Confucian concept of governmental legitimacy, and demonstrate the continuity of these concepts with contemporary Chinese political thought. Specifically, I will argue that legitimacy is based on the national myth, which offers a narrative account of the Party's origin, and ideological orthodoxy, which serves as an analogous concept to the Confucian understanding of virtue.

Chapter 3: The Crisis of Legitimation and the Demystification of Mao Zedong. This chapter traces the legitimation crisis that arose in the People's Republic after the death of Mao Zedong and the attempts at legitimation by Hua Guofeng and Deng Xiaoping. I will explain the strategic ways in which the Third Plenum of the Eleventh Party Congress and Twelfth Party Congress established Deng's legitimacy and set the stage for the later reform policies. I argue that Party meetings grounded the reforms in Mao's own instructions and the policies of the early Party, and that the 1981 release of the *Resolution on CPC History* served to delegitimate Mao Zedong and thus to loosen the ideological constraints on the reforms.

Chapter 4: The Thirteenth Party Congress and the Primary Stage of Socialism. This chapter reviews the theoretical impasse the reformers reached in the mid-1980s in establishing a market-oriented society. I argue that the reformers sought to legitimate the reform agenda by redefining the primary commitment to socialism within the society during the Thirteenth Party Congress in presenting the doctrine of the "primary stage of socialism."

Chapter 5: The Fourteenth Party Congress: Transition to a "Socialist Market Economy." This chapter documents the tensions that arose in the wake of the reforms in regard to the increased democratic expectations and the increasing prosperity of the nation, as well as the conservative campaign against "peaceful evolution." I argue that Deng Xiaoping was able to take a more aggressive role in seeking to undermine opponents of the reforms due to the successful legitimation of the reforms, and that the documents of the Fourteenth Party Congress refocused China's national agenda by introducing the concept of a "Socialist Market Economy."

Chapter 6: Chinese Political Discourse and the Rhetoric of Legitimacy. This chapter summarizes the progression of the strategy of legitimation, and the role of rhetorical action in establishing the ideological orthodoxy of the reform agenda. I will reexamine the utility of a rhetorical perspective on political legitimation, and summarize what is revealed about human communication generally by this analysis.

2 The Mythical and Ideological Dimensions of Political Legitimacy

As we noted earlier, the ways and means of power are of primary importance in understanding human social and political life. Since Max Weber's groundbreaking discussion of governmental authority, social scientists have engaged in an ongoing discussion of the nature of authority and leadership.[1] In this chapter, I hope to contribute to this discussion by establishing the twin rhetorical bases of legitimacy in China, the national myth and ideological orthodoxy. The national myth provides a sense of the historical place of the governing structures, contributing to the self-identity of the Chinese nation, while the emphasis on ideological orthodoxy provides stability and unity in the face of change and factional battles. Further, I will argue that these two rhetorical bases have pre-Republican counterparts; the doctrine of the Mandate of Heaven provided a sense of historical identity, while virtue served as a surrogate indicator of the legitimacy of Emperors. In Communist China, the retelling of the epic of the Chinese revolution provides the historical grounding, and ideological orthodoxy guarantees just rule.

One recent model of rhetorical legitimacy rests on the work of Jürgen Habermas, who contends that legitimation is a communicative process geared toward the maintenance of mass loyalty.[2] Legitimacy is when a political decision can "be made independently of the concrete use of force and of the manifest threat of sanctions, and can be regularly implemented even against interests of those affected."[3] Legitimacy is based on sociological motivations, which are shaped through "the internalization of symbolically represented structures of expectations."[4] This interpretive model argues that claims to legitimacy are subject to contest or verification within a communicative process. Without a communicative process of verification, there is no legitimacy.

Habermas argues that claims to legitimacy, in the realm of "practical questions," are derived from and must be consistent with the normative evaluations generated by the society. The moral basis for claims to legitimacy are presupposed by those who enter into legitimating and rationalizing discourse.[5] These norms not only reflect the societal values within the society; however, they also help to shape the dominant values. The rhetoric of legitimation is not alien to its culture, but rather enacts the deepest values, beliefs, and attitudes of that culture. In this sense, the politics of a culture reveal the true inner dynamics of that culture. The transcendence that causes one to ascribe loyalty to a regime is due to the intersubjective rationality, which takes the place of traditional worldviews in articulating a transcendent value system.

Habermas defines a legitimation crisis as a crisis of identity, in which the legitimizing system "does not succeed in maintaining the requisite level of mass loyalty."[6] In a legitimation crisis, the relationship between justificatory rhetoric and truth is severed. The rhetorical framework that subordinates individual interests to that of society has been tattered, no longer providing compelling reasons to abdicate one's own interests in favor of a transcendental interest.

While Habermas's work is a valuable contribution to an understanding of the processes of legitimation in modern Western societies, we must acknowledge some severe limitations of his analysis for the specific crisis of legitimation that sprang up in China during the period of economic reforms. One of these limitations is Habermas's clear focus on legitimation crisis in advanced capitalism, a crisis that he posits will eventually lead to some form of postcapitalist state. It seems self-evident that if differing societies have different "expectations" generated by differing value systems, rhetorical claims to legitimation will also vary across cultural, national, and social boundaries.[7]

I think that a more serious weakness of Habermas's model, and indeed, many Western models of legitimacy, is the innate presumption of an inevitable progression from traditional or charismatic legitimation to legal-rational systems of legitimation. Western analysis has tended to view Weber's first analysis of political legitimation through an interpretive framework of Marxist progression, and thus we see the legal-rational basis of legitimation as the most progressive form of governance. Traditional value systems and legitimizing discourse are seen as merely vestiges of feudalism on modern, complex societies. These assumptions must be reconsidered. Habermas himself acknowledges the weaknesses of the social sciences in fulfilling the role of a worldview,[8] and that his model of intersubjective rationality remains purely theoretical, since there is little available evidence of actual occurrence.[9] Moreover, how are we to account for political structures that do not allow for the discursive conditions that Habermas sees as vital to the legitimating process? Or regimes which seem, to Western eyes, to have lost all credibility because of ruthlessness or cruelty?

While it is true that the processes of secularization and modernization often diminish the role of tradition in evaluating the legitimacy of governments, it seems doubtful that modern societies will irrevocably eliminate the role of traditional belief systems in establishing legitimacy.[10] In fact, some scholars argue that modern secular legitimizing systems are inadequate in generating societal consensus. Robert Bellah, for example, argues that secular legitimizing systems "even when successful . . . seem to generate a surprising amount of public cynicism and a failure of civic commitment."[11]

Other authors have illustrated this inadequacy as well. It is clear that modern legitimating systems, once in place, are not safe from traditional critique. For example, Donald Rice has argued that in spite of the Western Marxist ideology of Fidel Castro, much of Castro's legitimacy rests on his close identification with José Martí, the influential nineteenth-century Cuban intellectual.[12] The rise of Islamic fundamentalism also demonstrates the instability of modernist legitimating discourse. D. Ray Heisey and J. David Trebing argue that the Iranian Revolution usurped the ideological primacy of modernization.[13] Specifically, the modernist ideology of the Shah's regime was successfully challenged by an ideology grounded in Iranian cultural history and religious authority. The authors argue that an existing legitimation crisis in Iran was unsuccessfully negotiated by the Shah's regime, making it vulnerable to the popular power of the Islamic Republic. Both of these examples illustrate the way in which vast political changes are legitimized by rhetorically creating alternatives to a secular, liberal modernism.

The key component we gain from Habermas's model, however, is the concept of practical rationality rooted in discourse. Other authors have argued that legitimacy can be explained in these terms. Thomas Luckmann, for example, argues that legitimation rests in "intersubjective action," or the rhetorical dynamics between those who exercise power and those who are subject to such power.[4] "The roots of legitimating processes are to be found in human social action, by justifying what is in the terms of what should be."[15] According to Luckmann, the processes of legitimation are linguistic and iconographic articulations; in other words, rhetorical activity.

Luckmann contributes to a broader understanding of legitimacy when he argues that "action is a project into the future. It is based on an articulation of what is the case now and an expectation of what should be the case later."[16] To clarify, the legitimation of policies (or regimes, or rulers) rests on a clear articulation of the present circumstances and the anticipated future state of affairs. When this link is made, the policies and agendas are made to seem compelling, transcendent, and morally worthy. Legitimacy rests in large part on a compelling vision of the future, or an eschatology.

I believe that we can better account for the narrative rationality of both Habermas and Luckmann by introducing the concept of national myth. I define a national myth as a narrative that explains and affirms the social identity of a people. John David Starr refers to "national myth," or a "retelling of history in order to depict the origins and development of a nation . . . and its place in the world in a way that coincides with the self-image of its founders and leaders."[17] Rhetorical scholars have long noted the legitimating power of mythic language.[18]

The rhetorical power arising from a national political myth is due to the unarticulated values of the culture fused to the specific power relationships of the society.[19] These "unarticulated values" of a culture are often inherent in the eschatological vision of the national myth. Walter Fisher helps us to understand that the narrative nature of the myth means that the "practical rationality" of the myth is subject to confirmation or disconfirmation on the basis of fidelity or coherence.[20]

The national myth provides a national and social identity for a nation and its people, thereby establishing the transcendence necessary for legitimation. The myth establishes an identity for a people based on their most salient values, an identity distinct from other nations.[21] National identity then serves to proscribe and restrict action and policy. Our actions as a political body must somehow be distinct from the actions of other political bodies, or our identity is meaningless.

In referring to a legitimating narrative as a myth, we make no judgment as to the truthfulness of the myth. We will presume that the truthfulness of any myth is determined by the "intersubjective action," referred to both by Habermas and Luckmann. As competing versions of the national myth interact, one or the other will gain or lose mass loyalty based on the perceived needs and goals of the populace. Presumably, each will have some basis in historical fact.

One contribution this concept makes to our understanding of political legitimation is that it locates the values of the nation within the expressed national myth. As different nations have different myths, the legitimating mechanisms will vary. The legitimating appeals of the United States will be critiqued upon the very foundations of the national myth, as Martin Luther King, Jr., critiqued existing power structures by using the analogy of an uncashed check, or promissory note written to American blacks that had not been honored.

The national identity is sometimes driven as much by a desired future as it is by an assumed past. Marxist nations in particular define national identity by the achievement of an ultimate goal.[22] An example of a practical application of the difference between the "rational" authority of the West and "eschatological" authority of many Marxist nations will help to clarify this argument. Western societies protect speech, even dangerous speech, because of a belief in the rules of society. There are no clearly defined goals, other than the maintenance of the rules. Any vision of the future can be offered, as long as the rules and procedures governing the society are maintained. Thus, a political party that envisions the wholesale reconstitution of society is not seriously questioned, as long as it pledges to maintain the system of democratic rules in place.

Marxist societies, on the other hand, suppress dissent based on the fact that the *goal* of society is being questioned. Occasionally, the structures and institutions (rules and procedures) that maintain an orderly society can be set aside, but only as long as the eventual goal of the society is not questioned. T. H. Rigby cites the example from the 1978 Soviet Constitution, which states that "enjoyment by citizens of their rights and freedoms must not be to the detriment of the interests of society or the state," interests that are defined tele-ologically, according to the goals of society.[23] In addition, in a nation such as China, which has no clearly defined processes of succession, the legitimation of any one leader must be based on something other than adherence to a process. The legitimacy of successors to leadership must articulate and identify with the perceived ends of the state.

Because Marxist societies are in large part driven by visions of the future, and are not regulated by procedural rules, great injustices can and do occur with little lasting damage to the credibility of the regime. Chairman Mao's axiom that "a revolution is not a dinner party" summarizes this perspective: great injustices and loss of life can occur for the sake of the ultimate cause, the revolution. Stalin's purges, the Soviet invasion of Czechoslovakia, and the Cultural Revolution demonstrate vividly the ability of a regime to deflect criticism on the grounds that the actions were necessary "for the sake of the revolution."

Any rhetorical attempt to gain legitimacy is also a critique of the existing power relationships. As Luckmann argues, "Legitimation as a process of making sense of power implies its corollary, a process of making nonsense of power, or making sense of a different distribution of power."[24] Thus, the process of legitimation is both an act of affirmation and an act of subversion.[25] Different and competing versions of the national myth, then, lead to corresponding social changes. The national myth, then, can account for radical changes in governing structures with little violence done to the underlying myth. Steven Sangren argues that in the Chinese context, at least, contradictory affirmations can exist simultaneously with little tension: "Simply put, in Chinese thought, history is capable of simultaneously authenticating contradictory models of power."[26] History can validate the legitimacy of a number of competitors to the throne, and none have an absolute claim.

This provides us with a beginning point from which to study the legitimation of agendas and movements, specifically, the Chinese economic reforms. So far, we have established that the national myth, with its attendant eschatological vision, is a vital tool of legitimation, establishing the very identity of the body politic. If this is so, then it is clear that a national myth restricts the range of policy options available to that nation. To return to the subject of this study, we see that in order to implement the reform policies, the Chinese Communist Party had to reconstruct the dominant political myth to a version that would allow room for the nation to experiment with quasi-capitalistic practices. To explore this in more detail, we will turn to a more focused examination of the Chinese national myth, and demonstrate the differences between legitimation rhetoric in China and that of other nations.

The dominant Chinese national myth, which we will refer to as the "myth of liberation," shared by both Taiwan and the People's Republic since the early part of the twentieth century, is a heroic epic, in which courageous leadership united with the power of the masses to overthrow corrupt governmental structures and dynasties. As noted above, this myth provided a transcendental value system whereby individual interests were subjected to the needs of the nation. We will examine two elements that merit close attention; the heroic plot and the mythic characters that serve as authorizing figures.

The plot of the myth of liberation is that China has been freed from the poverty, feudalism, and corruption that destroyed the once-great nation through the heroic efforts of political and leadership and the energies of the masses. One day China will be reunited, and will stand among the world's most modernized, prosperous, and important nations. What distinguishes the myth of Taiwan from the People's Republic of China (PRC) version is that the Taiwanese mark the Revolution of 1911 and the rise of the Kuomintang as the ultimate watershed in Chinese history.

In the Communist version, however, the Revolution of 1911 was a failed revolution and the Kuomintang but a step on the road to the Chinese Communist Party, which would prove to be the ultimate liberator of the Chinese nation. Although it is true that the CCP has demonized the Kuomintang, and vice versa, the Chinese Communist worldview prevents the absolute repudiation of the Kuomintang, because to do so would be to eliminate a key plank in the CCP's claim to progressive legitimacy. This worldview depicts the Communist Party as the spiritual successor to all of the progressive movements of the last hundred years, and as such, as inheritor of the legitimacy of those movements. Mao summed up this vision of history in 1939:

> If we trace China's bourgeois-democratic revolution back to its formative period, we see that it has passed through a number of stages in its development: the Opium War, the War of the Taiping Heavenly Kingdom, the Sino-Japanese War of 1894,

the Reform Movement of 1898, the Yi Ho Tuan (Boxer) Movement, the Revolution of 1911, the May 4th Movement, the
Northern Expedition, and the war of the agrarian revolution.
The present War of Resistance against Japan is yet another
stage, and is the greatest, most vigorous and most dynamic
stage of all . . . each stage in the development of the revolution
has its own distinguishing characteristics. But the most important feature differentiating them is whether they came before or
after the emergence of the Communist Party.[27]

For Mao, the CCP was the culmination of decades of progressive movements. Just as the doctrine of the Mandate of Heaven
traced the mantle of righteous authority through different dynastic
structures, the doctrine of historical progression traces it through
different revolutionary movements. The establishment of the CCP
was the fulfillment of the "mandate" of history. Thus, the legitimacy of the Party was in large part based on its role in history as the
apex of the struggle against oppression.

What makes this historical accounting "mythic" is that it does
more than just trace historical movements. Rather, it forms the self-
image of the Chinese nation, demonstrating that the values of the
society (egalitarianism, modernization, and prosperity) are ultimate
values grounded in the very progression of history. Finally, the myth
demonstrates how the the present government is the fulfillment of
those values.

The rhetorical power of a "history," then, is one of its most
and intriguing features. The logic behind these historical constructions is generally opaque to those who produce it: "It is precisely the
taken-for-granted authority of historical argument that constitutes
its ideological or mystifying power."[28] One cause of the authority
attributed to historical accounts is that they are self-mystifying.[29]
By hiding authority relationships in the veils of history, the social
construction of those relationships is veiled, thus making it more difficult to contradict the power relationships as manifested. When the
human genesis of histories is forgotten, the ideological dimensions of
that historical account are also obscured.

Kenneth Burke argues that "mystery," or that vague and unde-
finable sense that the hierarchies and social orders that exist are just
and right, is a process of our linguistic representations of reality. For
Burke, economic and social hierarchies are imbued with mystery
when their origins are linked with the divine. Mystery serves not

only to persuade people to accept certain hierarchical relationships, but also to maintain these distinctions by fogging the actual relationships behind objects of reverence through language:

> For, once a believer is brought to accept mysteries, he will be better minded to take orders without question from those persons whom he considers authoritative. In brief, mysteries are a good grounding for obedience . . . for in Earthy symbolicity, 'reason' will be closely associated with *rule*.[30]

When one set of institutions is replaced by another, one mystery has been replaced with another. Since hierarchy is inevitable, and symbolism itself produces mystery, mystery will always accompany human organization. Mythical histories establish authority and legitimacy, in short, by maintaining the mystery of leadership.

The mystery, or transcendence, that is established through historical narratives is what makes the status quo (or alternatives to the status quo) so compelling. This illustrates the quasi-religious concepts often underlying political institutions. In Confucian societies, as well as in modern inheritors of Confucian legacies, social orderings relate in some sense to the divine:

> Confucian philosophy makes explicit that which is merely implied by the idiom of *ling* (mystery): History necessarily authenticates cosmic order. . . . In Confucian ideology, history is held to manifest the hierarchical ordering of the cosmos, the workings of *yin* and *yang*, and, most important, the charisma of the properly ordered state.[31]

In the Peoples' Republic, the amount of direct impact of Confucian doctrines on the national consciousness is unclear, but it is clear that historical narrative continues to play a major role in the legitimation of the political order.[32]

The national myth is always ensconced in a historical setting, which dictates the mandate of History. The myth is populated by a cast of epic characters who have brought about historical change, such as Hong Xiuquan, leader of the Taiping Rebellion; Sun Yat-sen, the founder of the Nationalist (Kuomintang) Party; and Mao Zedong, chairman of the CCP. The Taiping Rebellion, the Boxer Rebellion, and the Kuomintang Revolution all held History's mandate. Popular leaders legitimate the structures associated with them and serve as authorizing figures by which later leaders and structures are legitimated. Sun, for example, is one historical figure to which both the Nationalist and the Communist governments continue to pay homage. The Belgian historian Simon Leys has written of Sun that:

> (T)he historical impact which he has had on the Chinese people as a whole is so important that even the adventurers who subsequently came to power, from Chiang to Mao, have always felt obliged to legitimize their own authority by claiming to be his spiritual heir.[33]

Sun's importance is not just in the actual historical and political role he played in the founding of the nation, but also in his mythic role, the character which justifies both the Kuomintang and the Communist governments. In fact, Sun was unable to effectively consolidate his rule except in a comparatively small region, nor was he able to establish the political mechanisms which would guarantee the continued dominance of the Kuomintang Party. Mythically, however, his failures are relegated to mere footnotes, in favor of the emphasis on his role as a valiant hero struggling to release China from the bonds of feudalism.

The role of the legitimating hero in establishing rule has frequently been noted. Lucian Pye argues that the most important cultural factor shaping Chinese politics and the ability to maintain a centralized authority system has been the "exaggerated ideal of the great man as leader—the emperor, generalissimo, chairman—who is an amplification of the Confucian model of the father as the ultimate authority in the family."[34] Not only did this figure serve as the ultimate authority, but this person became the 'authorizing figure' for all other potential leaders:

> Should any lesser figure wish to assert authority, he would have to protect himself by proclaiming even more loudly the greatness of the supreme authority. Those who were most vociferous in extolling Mao Zedong's greatness were usually advancing their own careers surreptitiously.[35]

Another example of the epic heros of the national myth are the students from the May Fourth Movement of 1919. The Beijing rallies, protesting the territorial concessions given to Western powers by the Imperial government in the Treaty of Versailles, are depicted as struggles to achieve self-determination and affect profound societal change. On the anniversary of the rallies in 1939, Mao said that:

> On this very day twenty years ago there occurred in China the great historical event known as the May 4th Movement, in which the students participated; it was a movement of tremendous significance. What role have China's young people played since the May 4th Movement? In a way they have played a vanguard role—a fact recognized by everybody except the die-hards.[36]

The efficacy of the May 4th Movement as an element of the national myth is attested to by Maurice Meisner, who argues that the movement "catalyzed the political awakening of a society which for so long had seemed inert and dormant, and thus provide(s) an appropriate drama for the nation, a drama of self-governance, of democracy, and of modernization."[37]

The greatest hero of the Chinese national epic, however, is Mao Zedong. Although the cult of Mao has been well documented by other scholars, it is valuable for our purposes to explore some of the rhetorical power of Mao's mythic image. Mao's reputation and legacy not only established his own legitimacy, but the legitimacy of the Party in large part rested on him. Mao's symbolic legacy has served both to advance and hinder the modernization process in China, depending on the ways in which Mao's legacy is appropriated. We will now explore the careful construction of Mao's mythic image in order to illustrate the importance of Mao in the legitimation process of the reform movement.

In a revealing essay on the beginnings of Mao's symbolic importance, appropriately entitled "Transfer of Legitimacy in the Chinese Communist Party: Origins of the Maoist Myth," William Dorrill states that in the official Party history compiled in 1945, "the successes and the failures of the CCP were invariably linked to the presence or absence of Mao Tse-tung's leadership . . . previous setbacks . . . were attributed to the 'errors' and ideological deviations of other CCP leaders."[38] The linkage of Mao with the success of the CCP would be developed more fully in later years, most completely during the decade of the Cultural Revolution.

Dorrill examines the manner in which legitimacy was transferred to Mao from the previously constituted leadership structure after 1934, when the Party was heavily defeated by Chiang Kai-shek's encirclement campaign against the Communist bases in Jiangxi Province. He argues that "Mao appears to have employed the device of historical revision to create an aura of legitimacy about his rule."[39] Key events in the CCP's campaign were reconstituted in the early 1940s, when many who could challenge the interpretation had died or been removed from the Party, so that Mao's role would be amplified in the successes of the Party. By the 1940s, "the revision of past history began to be blended into a myth of Mao's omniscient infallible leadership—a legend officially endorsed in the Central Committee's 1945 resolution on Party history."[40]

After the establishment of the People's Republic, the mythic image of Mao helped to stabilize the new government and legitimize the policies of the new government.[41] Frederick Teiwes has identified four distinct stages to Mao's authority, the early days of the revolution, the period from 1959–1965, the early Cultural Revolution, and the latter stages of the Cultural Revolution, when Mao's image began to slip.[42] In the early years of the revolution, virtually all modes of legitimacy reinforced Mao's image. From 1959–1965, senior officials challenged Mao's authority on legal-rational grounds, but their challenges were never very serious. Because of his great personal authority, Mao was able to implement policies opposed by other senior revolutionaries. The clearest example of this is Peng Dehuai's falling out with Mao at the Lushan conference of 1959, due to his outspoken criticism of Mao's Great Leap Forward policies.[43]

During the Cultural Revolution, from 1966–1971, the cult of Mao reached epic proportions. Many senior leaders privately questioned Mao's absolute authority, but few were willing to risk speaking out against it. Besides the well-known book of Mao's sayings, which served as a secular scripture for young Red Guards—during the reading of the *Red Book* no one could leave a room—there were other symbols of Mao's greatness and divinity. For example, one farmer wrote in the *Peking Review* in 1966 that "I learn dialectics (Mao's teachings) and grow bigger crops."[44] Other instances reveal that Mao's teachings resurrected people from the dead, enabled people to perform almost superhuman feats, and restored limbs.[45] Mao's legitimacy was charismatic in its purest form.[46]

Jung Chang, in her memoirs of growing up during the Cultural Revolution, writes about the tremendous appeal of the cult of Mao during this period:

Mao made himself more godlike by shrouding himself in mystery. He always appeared remote, beyond human approach . . . Mao, the emperor, fitted one of the patterns of Chinese history: the leader of a nationwide peasant uprising who swept away a rotten dynasty and became a wise new emperor exercising absolute authority. And, in a sense, Mao could be said to have earned his god-emperor status. He was responsible for ending the civil war and bringing peace and stability . . . It was under Mao that China became a power to be reckoned with in the world, and many Chinese stopped feeling ashamed and humiliated at being Chinese.[47]

The chaos of the Cultural Revolution also illustrates the rhetorical power of Mao's image. The launching of the Red Guards and the purging of loyal Party members at Mao's instructions turned the nation upside down, as many of the most capable administrators and cadres throughout the nation were imprisoned, killed, or removed from office. The prestige of Party membership was of little value, once Mao had declared that the Party was harboring "capitalist-roaders" and revisionists. Deng Xiaoping's own removal from office attested to the degree to which normal procedural channels could be bypassed by Mao's personal influence. Lin Biao's son is said to have commented that "Nothing is predictable. The chairman commands such high prestige that he need only utter one sentence to remove anybody he chooses."[48] Finally, after 1972, limited challenges to Mao's authority developed, although it was not until after Mao's death that the Party was able to begin to extricate itself from Mao's personal charisma.

Mao's image provides the most compelling example of a mythic hero within China's national myth. Mao represented not only the Party, but came to represent the hopes and aspirations of the Chinese nation. The cult was maintained in large part by limiting all discussion of other senior Party leaders. Jung Chang writes:

the near total lack of access to information and the systematic feeding of disinformation meant that most Chinese had no way to discriminate between Mao's successes and his failures, or to identify the relative role of Mao and other leaders in the Communists' achievements.[49]

In spite of his verbal allegiance to Marxism, Mao clearly stood at the head of a nationalistic, rather than Communistic, movement, and is widely credited with restoring China's dignity. Mao stood atop the Gate of Heavenly Peace in 1949 and proclaimed that "The Chinese people have stood up," thus visually illustrating his point while further fusing his image with the national identity of the Chinese people. This tight fusion contributed to the very delicate situation faced by the Chinese leadership after Mao's death in attempting to eliminate Mao's lingering influence on national politics.

The mythic account and the epic heros of Chinese history perform the legitimating function of Confucian doctrine in prerevolutionary China. In Confucian China, dynastic legitimacy was based on the doctrine of the Mandate of Heaven, which held that it was Heaven which both upheld dynastic rule and precipitated dynastic change. The doctrine taught that each governing dynasty since China's founding had come to power as a result of the will of Heaven. The continuance of Heaven's favor on a particular ruler depended on wise and just rule, concern for China's population, and the conscientious performance of ritual duties on behalf of the nation. When these duties were left unfulfilled, it was said that Heaven had withdrawn its mandate, an event usually signaled by military defeats and natural disasters, such as earthquakes and famines. Once one dynastic structure fell, it was replaced with a new one.

One interesting implication of this doctrine is that it allowed for a progression of dynastic rule without undercutting the absolute authority of Heaven. When dynastic change occurred, it was not because Heaven was somehow unable to maintain its favorite ruling clan, but because the emperor had proven unworthy to rule. Although fierce battles accompanied dynastic change, after the dust had settled, everyone could agree that the usurption had occurred because Heaven had so decreed, thus providing for a progressive history of changes in leadership. There was no inconsistency in affirming that a regime had both received and lost the Mandate of Heaven. As Hok-lam Chan has noted, this doctrine is double-edged in that it not only provides the grounds for legitimacy, but also serves as a powerful instrument of criticism against rulers.[50]

An example of the withdrawal of the Mandate is the displacement of the Yin Dynasty by the Chou Dynasty. Duke Chou is said to have remarked to the Emperor, "Heaven, without pity, sent down ruin on the Yin dynasty. Yin having lost the Mandate of Heaven; we, the Chou, have received it. But I dare not say with certainty that our heritage will forever truly remain on the side of fortune . . . Those who have lost the mandate did so because they could not practice and carry on the reverence of their forefathers."[51]

The dynastic change from the Southern Qi Dynasty to the Liang Dynasty in the sixth-century A.D. provides another example of the attempt to redefine recent history to establish legitimacy. On seizing power, the new emperor proclaimed:

> Fate has brought the house of Qi to a conclusion; but it is a continuation, not an end, for in response to Heaven the Mandate has come to me, and I have no choice but to accept the responsibility . . . Tang stepped aside that Yu might succeed to the throne; the Han dynasty was supplanted by the ascendency of the Wei dynasty, which in turn gave way to the Jin and Song. Their legitimacy was rooted in the past, and they all, through the virtue of their rulers, gained control of the world.[52]

The revisionist nature of the doctrine of the Mandate of Heaven is clear, in that the discourse of political legitimacy was concerned with tracing the movements of history to illustrate the will of Heaven. History was the only means of understanding and interpreting Heaven's will. Steven Sangren argues:

> In contrast to much of the traditional Western thought, where ultimate authority is attributed to a transcendent power and is known by means of revealed truth, for China, history itself is the text through which heaven's order can be known. Consequently, the universal penchant of authority to seek to control history has been particularly imperative in China. It is in history that the state legitimates itself; and circularly, it is in the state that history and heaven's order are revealed.[53]

The 1949 completion of the revolution did not unseat all of the old traditions and understandings of authority. Teiwes argues that "the imperial tradition has had some influence on authority relations in post-1949 China. Traditional notions of the loyalty owed to emperors, especially the founders of dynasties, reinforced the charismatic basis of Mao's hold over the elite."[54] Yan Jiaqi, formerly director of the Institute for Political Science of the Chinese Academy of Social Sciences, in a reference to a common political culture between pre-Republican and Communist China, argues that over the several thousand years of China's history, no tradition has persisted longer than the existence of dynasties. None has shown greater inertia than that of the dynasties. Despite repeated and cataclysmic peasant wars, endless palace coups, the chaos of outlying territories, and invasions by foreign ethnic groups, nothing has been able to break the dynastic cycle.[55]

The inertia behind the dynastic system manifests itself not only in the structures that develop, but also in the discourse of legitimation. The rhetoric of legitimation remains strikingly consistent, in spite of the violent usurpation of previous power relationships. Sangren argues that the same situation exists for the Nationalist government in Taiwan: "Both Nationalist and imperial states employ history as a primary rhetoric of legitimacy in characteristic Chinese fashion . . . The government has resurrected many of the forms of imperial legitimating ritual."[56]

The Confucian doctrine of the displacement of one dynasty by another accords with the historical progression of Chinese Marxist theory. Starr argues that "Marxism has provided the basic framework for this reinterpretation with its view of history as moving through broad stages."[57] Historical progression performs the same function as the Mandate of Heaven in ancient China. In classical thought, the Mandate provided justification for the displacement of dynasties. In New China, the doctrine of historical progression provides justification for the replacement of old structures by more just and humane political and economic orders. The Communist government has sought to legitimate the radical changes in Chinese society by retelling the national history and linking the history with the inevitable progression of history.

I have argued that besides providing a historical account of the emergence of the governmental structures, the mythic narrative contains an eschatological vision. It is this eschatological orientation that provides for hope and perseverance in the face of governmental nightmares. The source of this hope is a sure and certain conviction that just around the next corner is a just society. Lucian Pye argues that:

No matter what nightmare they (the Chinese) have just survived, they are always ready to proclaim that they are on the threshold of a new day that is certain to bring miracles of national accomplishment . . . All the broken promises of their past leaders are forgotten as they accept unquestioningly the new leader's vision of a bright tomorrow.[58]

The Chinese Communist Party has provided its own version of this eschatology. In this view, not only China, but all nations, will be socialistic and modernistic. Mao Zedong articulated the eschatological vision of the CCP in no uncertain terms:

In the future no country, whether it be Britain, the United States, France, Japan, Germany, or Italy, will have any place for capitalists, and China will be no exception. The Soviet Union is a country which has already established socialism, and beyond all doubt the whole world will follow its example. China will certainly go over to socialism in the future; *that is an irresistible law* (italics mine).[59]

The eschatology is never seriously questioned, because to the Chinese Communist Party, it is the inevitable result of history. In another speech, Mao declared that "if anyone asks why a Communist should strive to bring into being first a bourgeois-democratic society and then a socialist society, our answer is: we are following the inevitable course of history."[60] Thus, the progression of history is as clear and as inevitable as the transfer of the mandate of heaven. Just as Heaven's will was absolute, so historical progression is absolute. In this sense, then, the Mandate of Heaven is still the legitimating force in Chinese politics. The impersonal deity of Heaven has been replaced by the impersonal deity of History, to be sure, but History's mandate still stands firm. The maintenance of this doctrine, though, depends on a careful retelling of history so that the continuity is clear. The "mystery" within the national myth, then, lies in the quasi-divine nature of historical progression.

The retelling of the myth of revolution is a reminder of the fulfillment of history. The Marxist–Maoist version of Historical Progression contains the essence of the doctrine of the Mandate of Heaven. There are two practical rhetorical consequences to this retelling of history. The first is that the retelling of the myth reminds the audience of the ultimate goal of history—the establishment of a utopian state, thus grounding the values of the society in history itself, and legitimating the role of the Party in society. The second is that by reconstructing recent history—emphasizing some elements, obscuring others—policies can be legitimated as in accordance with the very identity of the nation and the people. Thus, the retelling of history is a projection into the future, a prophecy of the state of society in the future.

So far, we have seen that there are two main elements of the Chinese national myth: the inevitable progression of history and epic characters who serve as authorizing figures, such as Sun Yat-sen, the May Fourth students, and Mao Zedong. Further, we have seen that the national myth rhetorically functions successfully because it is consonant with the ancient doctrine of the Mandate of Heaven. One other element of Chinese political consciousness must be explored to gain a complete picture of the legitimating discourse of the economic reforms, the role of ideology in rhetorical legitimation.

In Confucian doctrine, the virtue of the emperor and his subjects served as prerequisites for the mandate of Heaven. Virtue guaranteed longevity. Virtue, to the dynastic emperors, meant the moral qualities and ritual correctness necessary to lead the nation in an enlightened manner. When the rulers acted in ways that revealed a lack of virtue, the right to rebel was guaranteed by the doctrine of the Mandate of Heaven.

To the Chinese Marxists, however, virtue refers to the inherent moral qualities of the proletariat, qualities that Benjamin Schwartz has identified as "selflessness in the 'service of the people,' lack of self-interest, austerity, singularity of purpose, implacable hostility to the forces of evil . . . etc."[61] These qualities of the proletariat are not merely inner character qualities, however; they are a function of correct ideology, and orthodoxy is a function of class structure. To the Chinese Communists, only the proletariat can be trusted to see things as they truly are, and thus only the proletariat can be trusted to be orthodox.[62] By ideology, I mean a set of doctrines and values that are currently endorsed by the Party leadership. Although ideology has several functions, the most important function for our purposes is its rhetorical power of legitimation.[63]

To the Chinese Communist Party, ideology is not merely an intellectual abstraction; rather, it is a settled worldview and morality. Correct ideology brings forth moral behavior; incorrect ideology brings forth immoral behavior. The linkage of ideology to morality has tremendous consequences for political life. Harry Harding argues that "there are strong tendencies in Chinese political culture to see politics in highly moralistic terms, [and thus] to deny the pos-

sibility of a loyal political opposition."[64] To the CCP, political opposition is not grounded in legitimate disagreement over issues; it is
grounded in a lack of character. Variance with orthodoxy is not an
honest disagreement over policy issues; it is treason. Since ideology
is so strongly linked to morality, the promotion of alternative ideologies is absolutely forbidden. Pye argues that the Chinese are more
willing to permit hypocrisy than an open challenge to the established ideology.[65] Anne Norton argues that Marxist regimes share
with liberal Western regimes a pretension to universality, which
often treat dissidence as a type of insanity.[66] Since the ideology is
self-evidently true and just and moral, those who disagree must not
be rational.

Since correct ideology is necessarily moral and true, it becomes
the ultimate requirement for governmental legitimacy. The virtuous
demonstrate their moral authority to rule by a steadfast adherence to
correct ideology. In the Chinese political structure, ideology has a
decisive rhetorical power, for in identification of a person's ideological standing, there is a concomitant identification of legitimacy.
The dissident journalist Liu Binyan has remarked that "Inside the
Communist Party, whoever controls theory (in other words, whoever
defines orthodox ideology) has 'truth' and gains decisive power in any
political struggle."[67] The process of defining ideological orthodoxy
has tremendous consequences, in that the final definition identifies
legitimate leadership within China.

The CCP feels safe with this criterion for leadership because of
an unshakeable faith in the infallibility of ideology. Ideology is not
derived from personal bias or subjectivity, but rather an absolute
knowledge grounded in Marxism-Leninism. As Hua Guofeng
attested:

> Such is our optimism. It is based on scientific grounds. Pro-
> vided that we know more about Marxism-Leninism and the
> natural sciences, in short, more about the laws of the objec-
> tive world, and make fewer mistakes of a subjectivist kind, we
> are sure to attain our goals in revolution and construction.[68]

Marxism–Leninism attains the same absolute standards of
truth as do the natural sciences in this scheme. Political decisions
are based on a scientific, objective basis, and policies are seen as
derived directly from the objective reality of orthodoxy. Variance
from orthodoxy can only be explained by reference to someone will-

fully obscuring the truth of the objective situation, and it is for this reason that punishment for dissent is often severe.

Perhaps in what can only be described as pure irony, Deng Xiaoping himself sees ideology in the same manner, even though he has often been at the receiving end of severe sanctions. Deng argues that "whether a correct political line can be implemented depends primarily on whether we have a correct ideological line."[69] However, it is not just the current leadership of China that believes in the infallibility of ideology. Many of the Chinese dissidents have absolute faith in another ideology, science. To the dissidents, science is absolute. To quote Yan Jiaqi again:

> Whatever the phenomena that emerge in the course of practice, no matter how new or hard to understand, all of them can be understood by science . . . Our fundamental attitude to the world around us is to admit that all phenomena, including those which are hard to understand, have objective existence . . . Science has always been the enemy of ambiguity and vagueness; only religion and mysticism try to enchant and intoxicate . . . from the standpoint of science, there is no concrete problem that cannot be solved. Of course the choice of goals, in itself, must depend on science.[70]

While Yan grants that scientific discussion must be open to debate, his uncritical attitude toward the absolutes of scientific inquiry reflect the same faith in precision and orthodoxy that characterize the top leaders of the CCP. His remark that science must determine political goals betrays the ideological nature of science. In commenting on the pervasiveness of a rigid stress on ideological consensus, Lucian Pye has argued that "The Chinese have always felt profoundly uncomfortable, dissatisfied, and threatened whenever their politics has not been characterized by a dominant hierarchy and a single ideology."[71] Politics, in the Chinese worldview, is sufficient to handle all problems; thus the great conflicts during the Cultural Revolution over the "red versus expert" question. At least during that decade, expertise was merely a bourgeois tool of oppression; with the correct ideology, expertise was unnecessary. Pye argues further that "no other people in history have had as great a need to dress up their politics in formal ideological trappings."[72]

At least some of the reason for the inordinate emphasis on ideological orthodoxy can probably be traced to the fear the Chinese have of factionalism and chaos. Pye argues that "The Chinese are generally convinced that disaster will follow if brothers fight, if villages have feuds, or if there are factions in their elite politics."[73] While this might be an overstatement of the case, it does seem true that by emphasizing ideological orthodoxy on all levels of society, the Chinese are attempting to minimize the chances of disruption later on. This may account for the destructiveness of the military crackdown on the 1989 Tiananmen student demonstrators. By a forceful response, the authorities signaled their impatience with any political ambiguity.

Because of the necessity for ideology to be ultimate and unchanging, policy changes or theoretical turnabouts are often ignored or downplayed. Helmut Martin argues that "The ideological orientation adopted at any particular moment drew its legitimation from an orthodox theory, proclaimed to be eternal and immutable, which denied the contradictory developments or controversial about-faces that had in fact taken place and indeed, had produced the given situation."[74] If the changing nature of state ideology were to be constantly revised and this revision admitted to, the very security that ideology provides would be found lacking.

The prevailing standard of orthodoxy since 1949, of course, is Mao Zedong Thought. This is normally to be found in the *Selected Works of Mao Zedong* as well as the little red book popularized during the Cultural Revolution.[75] These texts have served throughout the Communist period as the canon for orthodoxy, although it is not altogether rare when contradictory opinions can be grounded in Mao's works.

Just as the Mantle of Heaven went to the virtuous, so legitimacy in contemporary China rests on those with the correct ideology. The mantle of moral legitimacy rests upon the party that possesses the qualities or the virtues of the proletariat. Mao Zedong's insistence on the 'mass line' was a legitimate extension of this, as it was only those with the experience of the peasants and workers who could possibly possess the moral qualities necessary to lead the nation. Regardless of whatever other motives Mao might have had, his purges of intellectuals and others were probably due to his conviction that those being purged could not possibly have the virtue necessary for leadership.

Ideological orthodoxy is also seen as a guarantee of the ability to bring actual tangible benefits to the populace. In much the same way that a Confucian Emperor was expected to exhibit a benevolent paternalism over the peasantry, so the Party is expected to be able to bring prosperity to the populace. Mao continually argued during the early years of the Revolution that the peasantry was the key to winning China, and that to achieve this, the Party had to provide tangible benefits to the peasants, such as land reform policies. In a conversation with the American reporter Edgar Snow, Mao said, "Whoever wins the peasants will win China."[76] The strategy of identification with the peasantry was a break from traditional Marxism, which postulated that it was the urban proletariat that would lead the revolution, and it was for this reason that Mao came into conflict with the Soviet Party.

Similarly, in a speech made at the conclusion of the Second National Congress of Workers and Peasants' Representatives in early 1934, Mao reiterated his conviction that the first task of the Party was to:

> convince the masses that we represent their interests, that our lives are intimately bound up with theirs . . . By linking the problem of the well-being of the masses with that of the revolutionary war, the comrades . . . are simultaneously solving the problems of revolutionary methods of work and of accomplishing their revolutionary tasks.[77]

Ralph Thaxton argues that this strategy was the key to the establishment of the New China:

> Inasmuch as the Chinese Communist Party derived its mandate to rule China from practices that validated much of what the peasants wanted by way of justice and order, it becomes possible to speak of the Chinese Revolution as a folk revolution, that is, as a revolution in the service of the humble folk. In the most fundamental sense, the CCP won by raising a protective shield before the peasant communities.[78]

To the leadership of the Chinese Communist Party, it seems clear that the CCP has inherited the mantle of just rule due to its virtue and moral qualities; in short, its ideology. Since the CCP is seen as embodying the virtues of the proletariat, then there are no alternatives to its command. Even young intellectuals who identify themselves with the early radicalism of the Party had not necessarily developed the important virtues. Mao said during the Chinese civil war:

the young intellectuals and students throughout the country must unite with the broad masses of workers and peasants and become one with them, and only then can a mighty force be created . . . There can only be one criterion, namely, whether or not he is willing to integrate himself with the broad masses of workers and peasants and does so in practice. If he is willing to do so and actually does so, he is a revolutionary; otherwise he is a non-revolutionary or a counter-revolutionary. . . . Some young people talk glibly about their belief in the Three People's Principles or in Marxism, but this does not prove anything. Doesn't Hitler profess belief in "socialism"? Twenty years ago even Mussolini was a "socialist"! . . . When we assess a person and judge whether . . . he is a true or false Marxist, we need only find out how he stands in relation to the broad masses of workers and peasants, and then we shall know him for what he is.[79]

With this understanding, then, it is easy to see why Mao launched the Cultural Revolution against those whom he perceived as bureaucratic usurpers of the Revolution. In Mao's thinking, there were those in the Party, even at the top levels of leadership, who did not possess the qualities of the proletariat, and their ideological errors could be disastrous, leading to the overthrow of the nation. To quote Schwartz again, "Mao . . . found that the CCP, both in its human composition and as an organizational structure, has failed at least for a time to embody the qualities of the 'dictatorship of the proletariat.'"[80] Just as virtue was required of emperors to maintain the mandate of Heaven, so ideological orthodoxy is necessary to maintain one's standing within the Communist Party. When Party members are found lacking in ideological commitments, their loyalty is suspect and they are stripped of responsibility.

Ideology thus assumes a tremendous rhetorical power within Chinese political life. Since ideological justifications serve as the primary basis for legitimate rule, all policy and personnel decisions must be framed within an ideological explanation. Since variance from ideological orthodoxy not only signals distortion of the true faith, but also heresy, all change must be accounted for within the preexisting ideology. Chinese politics assumes a conservative character, based on some previous standard of early radical policies. The radical consciousness of Mao was the standard by which orthodoxy was judged during the Cultural Revolution, and during the early post-Mao days, rightist deviation was taken to be the ultimate heresy. Those who fell out of favor were said to be "capitalist-road-ers" or "right deviationists." Even after the arrest of the Gang of Four, this radical, ultraleft clique was referred to as "typical representatives of the bourgeoisie inside the Party, unrepentant capitalist-roaders still travelling on the capitalist road and a gang of bourgeois conspirators and careerists."[81]

As a legitimating factor, ideology maintains its important role even when any particular orthodoxy is in the process of decay.[82] In the case of the Chinese economic reform movement, the specific ideological and theoretical backing for the newer policies have at times been ambiguous, untested, and in flux. However, the rhetorical force that comes with the mantle of orthodoxy has pushed the reforms forward, in spite of these weaknesses.

The functional parallels between the doctrine of the Mandate of Heaven and the contemporary national myth, as well as those between virtue and ideology, are the grounding for legitimacy in the People's Republic. The re-creation of history validates future policy, and hence legitimates whichever party can present the most compelling historical account. Virtue and ideology serve as indicators of the moral qualities of leaders.

The implications of this for our understanding of Chinese politics are enormous. In particular, the nature of the legitimacy crisis in China at the death of Mao Zedong becomes clearer. Not only had the epic hero of the national myth died, but the very ideological basis that the nation had presumed infallible during Mao's lifetime was undermined by the chaos of the ideological competition. The clear and undisputed truths on which the Cultural Revolution was launched had plunged the nation into chaos, and it seemed as if there was no end in sight.

Deng Xiaoping's return from the margins of ideological heterodoxy further clouded the clear ideological truths that had been taken for granted. The abstract philosophical battles over the criterion of truth took on a magnitude undreamed of in the West. Not only were the short-term consequences of the battles at stake, but ultimately, the future direction of the nation. In Chapter 3, we will turn our attention to the ideological and authority crisis immediately after Mao's death, and examine the subtle rhetorical campaign by Deng Xiaoping and the reform faction to move the nation off of the course plotted by the Great Helmsman.

3 The Crisis of Legitimation and the Demystification of Mao Zedong

1976 was a tumultuous year for China. Premier Zhou Enlai died in January and Mao Zedong the following September. The nation was left with no clearly recognized leader, and this caused bitter and at times violent competition among different factions within the governing Party. Perhaps even more profoundly, China felt the loss of a clear ideological and policy direction. The nation had willingly followed Mao into the Cultural Revolution, but was now recoiling from the horrors and the wanton violence of that decade and was beginning to tentatively question Mao's legacy to the Chinese people.

Deng Xiaoping reemerged in this leadership vacuum as a major voice within the Party, and quickly set the nation on a course of economic reform and expansion. In addition, it was clear to Deng and his reform-minded allies that the worldview inherited from Chairman Mao would not allow for the radical reforms he proposed. The national myth, as articulated by Mao, was that China's backwardness was due to the exploitive colonization of China by foreign powers. In order to implement the reforms, it was necessary to establish that China's backwardness was due to the nation's own withdrawal from economic growth and openness to the world.[1] How Deng and his reformist faction managed to negotiate the highly volatile struggle for legitimacy during this period, and how the ideological grounds necessary for the process of economic restructuring were established will be the focus of this chapter.

Earlier, I argued that political legitimacy in China has been based in large part on a compelling historical narrative and adherence to orthodox ideology. In this chapter, I will analyze the legitimation crisis that faced the reformers after Mao's death and argue that the early struggle for the legitimacy of the Deng regime and his economic reforms entailed the subtle transformation both of the national myth and ideological orthodoxy so as to accomplish two specific rhetorical tasks. The first task was to begin the long and careful process of delegitimating the Maoist vision and the excesses of the Cultural Revolution. This also meant the delegitimation of Mao's hand-picked heir to power, Hua Guofeng. The second task was to ground economic reform in the unfinished projects of the early Communist Party. By so doing, the reformers could argue that they were implementing the policy directions that Mao himself had urged. The remainder of this chapter demonstrates how these ideological strategies were established through the 1978 Third Plenum of the Eleventh Party Congress, the Twelfth Party Congress in 1982, and the 1981 *Resolution on CPC History*.

The Crisis of Legitimation and Modernization

There were at least three aspects of the legitimation crisis of the late 1970s: the indisputable elimination of Hua Guofeng's authority and Deng Xiaoping's reemergence to China's top leadership; the rise of the democracy movement in China's urban centers; and, perhaps even more fundamentally, the tensions that arose as a result of modernization. The scene was marked not only by factional tensions and rivalries festering in China's leadership structure, but also by battles over ideological orthodoxy. The fundamental certainty of the accepted textual basis for ideology, Mao's *Selected Works*, had been called into question once Marshall Lin Biao's aborted coup came to light in the early part of the decade. Lin, who had edited the first four volumes of the works of Mao Zedong and was largely responsible for Mao's personality cult, was allegedly killed in a plane crash while trying to escape after a conspiracy to overthrow Mao came to light in 1971. His death and subsequent renunciation thus cast doubt even on the textual basis for the Chinese ideology, Mao Zedong Thought. Since Lin had edited the authoritative collection of Mao's essays and speeches, and was subsequently shown to be a "counterrevolutionary traitor," what was to be made of the volumes that he had edited? It was difficult to believe that the editing of Chairman Mao's writings by a "counterrevolutionary traitor" would not in some fundamental way alter them.

This ideological crisis was exacerbated by at least three competing factions, led respectively by Hua Guofeng, the Gang of Four, and Deng Xiaoping. Each faction attempted to ground its version of ideological orthodoxy in the legacy of Mao and his thought.

On Mao's death in September of 1976, Hua Guofeng succeeded him as chairman of the Chinese Communist Party. Hua, whom Mao had personally elevated from a lower provincial position to national leadership, was able to assume power because the dying Mao had supposedly handwritten a note that said: "With you in charge, I am at ease."[2] Hua reinforced his identification with Mao by appointing himself editor of the fifth volume of Mao's *Selected Works*, attempting to establish his credentials as a theorist in the same manner as Lin Biao had done with the earlier volumes. In January of 1977, Hua proclaimed his allegiance to two principles soon to be known as the "Two Whatevers"; that the nation would follow whatever policies Mao had implemented and whatever instructions Mao gave. Besides attempting to identify himself ideologically with Mao, Hua stressed every possible point of comparison, even to the extent of combing his hair the same way as Mao had and attempting to keep control of Mao's remains through the building of Mao's mausoleum.[3]

Even as Hua stressed his identification with Mao, however, he found it necessary to counter some of the effects of Mao's later policies, such as the Cultural Revolution. The decade of the Cultural Revolution, 1966–1976, had been a disaster; millions of Chinese citizens, many of them loyal Party members, had been persecuted or even executed because of alleged crimes against the state.

While Hua Guofeng was struggling to establish himself as the rightful heir to leadership, the "Gang of Four," a politically powerful faction who had come to prosper during the Cultural Revolution, was actively competing with Hua for political power, as well as ideological orthodoxy, through media campaigns and wall posters. Although Hua held the formal titles of leadership, the Gang had supporters throughout the government, as well as the momentum of the previous ten years to sustain their claims to legitimacy. Significant elements of the Party and state bureaucracy owed allegiance to the Gang, and the ideology espoused by the Gang had the added benefit of a seeming consistency with Mao's own.

Hua cut short this rivalry by arresting the "Gang of Four" and charged them with crimes of treason a month after Mao's death, setting in motion a process of criticism that would inevitably lead to questions about Mao Zedong himself. Throughout their trials, the Gang protested innocence, and argued that they had only followed Mao's directives. Jiang Qing, Mao's wife and a key member of the Gang, argued in her trial that "I was Chairman Mao's dog. Whomever he told me to bite, I bit."[4] This sort of testimony progressively revealed Mao's own role in ordaining the terror of the period. As Mao's authority began to erode, however, so did Hua's, based as it was on Mao's handwritten affirmation.

In spite of the arrest of the Gang, though, the supporters of the Gang, dispersed throughout the Party and government bureaucracies, were not easily eliminated. Immediately after the arrest of the Gang, a campaign to criticize the four was begun in earnest throughout the nation. The campaign did not establish any answers to the many questions that remained as to orthodoxy. Hua based his orthodoxy on the "Two Whatevers" slogan, while the Gang rallied around the slogan "act in accordance with principles laid down." Both of the slogans promised continuity with Mao's own policies, but led to radically different interpretations, leading to a real confusion as to which faction actually represented Mao's own beliefs.

A related tension contributing to the legitimation crisis involved the reinstatement of Deng Xiaoping to high political office. Since joining the party while a student in France in the 1920s, Deng had been an active and influential member, serving as General Secretary of the Party in the 1950s, and was one of the few remaining members of the "Long March Generation," those who had been actively involved in revolutionary activity in the during the mythic Long March from Jiangxi to Yanan. However, Deng had been removed from office during the Cultural Revolution as a "capitalist-roader." After spending several years in a labor farm in remote Jiangxi Province, Deng returned to Beijing, but was again removed by Mao in the spring 1976 for his alleged support of the Qing Ming rallies commemorating Zhou Enlai. These rallies had became personal embarrassments to Mao, as they were characterized by open dissatisfaction with the course of the Cultural Revolution.

At the time of Mao's death, Deng was still out of favor and the nation was in the midst of a "criticize Deng Xiaoping" campaign.

The campaign was centered around charges that Deng was ideologically unorthodox; specifically, that Deng believed class struggle was over in China, that he wanted to restore capitalism, that he wanted to reverse the gains of the Cultural Revolution, and that he believed that China should import foreign techniques. Deng had indeed supplied ample evidence for the truthfulness of many of these charges.[5] Largely because of the Gang of Four, the campaign intensified after Mao's death, as the government urged the nation to continue Mao's struggle by "taking class struggle as the key link," and deepening the criticism of Deng.[6]

In spite of the campaign and the criticism, however, there was widespread popular support for Deng's reinstatement. Hua Guofeng found himself on the outside of this popular sentiment, as his insistence that Mao had made no mistakes during his final years meant that Mao was correct to dismiss Deng. In addition, the popular clamor for Deng's return cast a negative light on Mao Zedong himself. One analyst argues that "Many critical questions and issues were associated with his [Deng's] rise again. His return could not be accomplished without damage to Mao's image and to Hua's personal place in the party."[7] Deng's reinstatement would undermine the ideological campaigns waged against him as well as the prevailing national myth. Hua was unable to withstand the pressure from other top officials to reinstate Deng, and his own need for capable leaders, and by 1978, Deng was reinstated to top political posts.[8] The battle to define orthodoxy also heated up, as Deng's supporters launched a media battle over the norms of truth. Deng's dictum that "practice is the sole criterion of truth" became the banner under which reform-minded Party members banded together, against those defending the "Two Whatevers" standard.

The reformers attempted to strengthen their case by arguing that Mao himself had established that practice was the sole criterion of truth. As Schram argues:

> The validity of this proposition [practice is the sole criterion of truth] itself was justified, not merely by the argument . . . that it had *worked* in the past, but by the fact that it was in conformity with the utterances of Chairman Mao. In other words, it not only made good sense, but was doctrinally sound.[9]

Mao's often cryptic sayings, however, had been interpreted in a variety of ways, and Deng's interpretation was officially disputed.

By 1981, Deng's reformist faction had placed officials through-out the hierarchy. Besides an obvious infiltration of every level of government, Deng's strategy for undermining Hua's authority and power included subverting the ideological foundation of Hua's sup-porters. One Chinese analyst argues that "Deng's strategy of regain-ing power was through a circuitous route: eschewing a frontal bid for power, he set out to use his supporters to whittle away the ideolog-ical foundations of the Hua regime and to create a political atmo-sphere that enhanced his own prestige."[10] Having lost all but his for-mal titles, Hua resigned from his post as chairman of the Party at a 1978 Central Committee meeting, leaving Deng as the undisputed leader of China.

Although Deng's consolidation of power was strong among some Party stalwarts, the legitimacy of his rule was still open to question, both among lower-level Party cadres and the citizenry. Deng's return to power was seen by many as a blow to Mao, in that it was Mao who had cast him from power twice before. The pro-tracted ideological battles waged in the media seemed to be without resolution. Furthermore, Hua Guofeng's resignation in spite of Mao's explicit endorsement could not but raise uneasy questions as to the ways in which leadership was established in China. It seemed that Chinese political life was not altogether different from the court life of ancient China.

Deng's program to undo many of the Maoist economic poli-cies and reopen China to the outside world was inconsistent with Mao's version of the national myth. Where Mao had proclaimed that self-sufficiency and a policy of closure were necessary for Chinese regeneration, Deng and the reformers openly argued that openness and reliance on foreign help were vital to stimulate economic growth. Clearly, elements of the national myth that contributed to economic stagnation had to be cleared away for the reform agenda to proceed.

In addition to the ideological battles raging in Beijing, another significant tension within the society emerged from those portions of the population who were thoroughly disillusioned with Mao's legacy. Students and intellectuals were especially disenfranchised, especially those in Beijing. For the intellectuals who had suffered during the Cultural Revolution, a wholesale rethinking of the nature of Chinese politics was in order. Millions of citizens, including top Party officials, had been subjected to "struggle sessions," in which they were denounced and forced to confess their thought crimes against the Party. A powerful sense of hopelessness characterized those who had come of age during this period, later to be known as the "lost generation."[11]

In 1978, Wei Jingsheng posted a wall article entitled "The Fifth Modernization" in an area known as Beijing's "Democracy Wall." The poster declared that political reform must accompany the economic and technical modernizations that the government was pursuing. Intellectuals were assured that they had Deng Xiaoping's support in their criticism of the Cultural Revolution, as their calls for change seemed to strengthen his political hand. Soon, rallies were being held across China, the first stirrings of a democracy movement. Once the rallies seemed to threaten stability, however, Deng himself denounced them and called for harsh measures to quell the rallies. Wei Jingsheng was sentenced to fifteen years in jail for treason, but his article stood as a testament to the sentiments of many intellectuals.

Besides the factional struggles in Beijing and the public battle to control ideological orthodoxy, a third and more subtle difficulty underlay the crisis of legitimation, what Lucian Pye has referred to as the "authority crisis in modernization."[12] Pye argues that an "authority crisis" is engendered when "the cultural and psychological bases for the legitimacy of political power are radically undermined by the developmental process."[13]

In the Chinese case, several elements to this crisis can be clearly identified. The first of these is the psychological confusion that results when old institutions are replaced or lose their effectiveness. Pye cites the role of the socialization process within the family as a locus of confusion. In addition to this, traditional assumptions about China's preeminent place in the world were turned upside down, as greater exposure to technology and the outside world revealed China's relative poverty. Deng's campaign to introduce foreign technology and expertise seemed to turn the dogma of self-reliance taught by Mao on its head.

Thus, many of the ideological and mythical conclusions of previous years were severely questioned by significant portions of China's populace. The loss of ideological certainty, the fall of Hua Guofeng, and the rise of Deng Xiaoping and his reform movement all contributed to a sense of aimlessness in a nation accustomed to clearly articulated goals. The remainder of this chapter examines the nature of the rhetoric designed to undermine continued reliance on the Maoist model and to establish a new regime based on reforms.

I argue that the rhetoric of this period sought to alter the national myth and the prevailing orthodoxy, thus delegitimating Maoist policies and replacing them with a more reformist agenda.

The Third Plenum and Economic Modernization

Deng was restored to his previous posts in 1977, after writing a personal letter to Hua Guofeng pledging his support and confessing to mistakes made in 1975. Although still subordinate to Hua, Deng thus reentered the political stage on which he would soon unseat Hua. Finally, at the Third Plenum of the Eleventh Central Committee in 1978, the reformist faction gained decisive theoretical and organizational victories. It is probable that the organizational victories from the Third Plenum were much more significant than any wholescale repudiation of ideology.[14] The Third Plenum did, however, lay important groundwork for the later reformation of the national myth and orthodoxy.

The Third Plenum turned out to be a watershed meeting, "a crucial turning point of far-reaching significance in the history of our Party," in the words of the 1981 *Resolution on CPC History*.[15] Several significant events occurred that would have a great impact on the changing ideological orthodoxy. Hua maintained chairmanship of the Party, but several of Deng's supporters were sent to the Politburo. More important, Deng was able to demonstrate his control over the nation's agenda, reappropriate the Four Modernizations, a campaign largely identified with Zhou Enlai, as his own contribution, and deal a final blow to the "Two Whatevers" doctrine. The Communique released by the Central Committee detailing the work of the plenum was widely released and studied throughout the nation.[16] The Communique endorsed Deng's dictum on "practice as the sole criterion of truth," establishing Deng's preeminence in defining orthodoxy.

The Third Plenum's most important rhetorical function was to legitimate a change of focus away from class struggle toward economic modernization. This move reversed both Mao's teachings and Hua's proclamation at the 1977 Eleventh Party Congress to "take class struggle as the key link."[17] At the Eleventh Party Congress, Hua had not only stressed total obedience to this dictum, but he had also proclaimed the successful conclusion of the Cultural Revolution and called for further Cultural Revolutions, as they became necessary. Economic need was barely mentioned at all. The over-whelming emphasis on the shift to economic modernization at the Third Plenum, only two years later, showed Hua Guofeng to be over-whelmed by Deng's influence and agenda.

Rhetorically, the shift was legitimated by altering orthodoxy and subsequently altering the national myth; specifically, Mao's role in that myth. Mao and his teachings could not be directly attacked, however. Still only two years since Mao's death, it was too early to disown Mao, and it was imperative that the reforms be seen as consistent with Mao's thought:

> In the early years after the founding of the People's Republic, especially after the socialist transformation was in the main completed, Comrade Mao Tsetung instructed the whole Party time and again to shift the focus of our work to the field of the economy and technical revolution. Under the leadership of Comrade Mao Tse-tung and Comrade Chou En-lai, our Party did a great deal for socialist modernization and scored important achievements. But the work was later interrupted and sabotaged by Lin Piao and the 'gang of four.'. . . The session holds that the fundamental policy put forth in the report On the Ten Major Relationships which Comrade Mao Tsetung made in 1956, . . . is an objective reflection of economic law and also an important guarantee for the political stability of society. This report still is significant for guidance today.[18]

The Communique argued that the basis of post-Mao restructuring was Mao's own directions and policy. Lin Biao and the Gang of Four were blamed for the Cultural Revolution as well as the skewed economic policies later identified with Mao. Lin and the Gang, having been identified as enemies of the Party, became convenient scapegoats for Mao's failed policies.

In addition, the historical stage also required an important shift: "The general task put forward by our Party for the new period reflects the demands of history and the people's aspirations and represents their fundamental interests."[19] The historical progression of the national myth dictated that the Party's focus be turned to modernization, another stage in the inevitable history of China. This shift to economic modernization reflected a new stage in the Party's history, one just as important as the early political revolution. This "technical revolution" would be characterized by the same progress that the political revolution attained. The eschatological vision shifted from a utopian communist state to "a modern, powerful socialist country before the end of this century."[20]

Ideological orthodoxy itself was altered by the Communique's proclamation of a shift away from class struggle as the "key link" of Party work, in Mao Zedong's words. The document asserted that the goal of the socialist revolution was not class struggle, but economic development. Agricultural development was declared the specific target on which the nation would focus. According to the Communique, grain production was to be taken as key link. The heros of this historical stage were to be policy makers and technical specialists, rather than military leaders: "The best contribution to the thirtieth anniversary of the founding of our People's Republic will be to shift the emphasis of our work to socialist modernization and to achieve the expected success next year."[21]

Ideological orthodoxy was also secured at the Third Plenum by the official repudiation of Hua's "Two Whatevers" policy. The Communique never specifically mentioned the policy, but in its endorsement of Deng's slogan that "practice is the sole criterion of truth," it was clear that Hua had lost the battle to define orthodoxy. The document proclaimed that Deng's thesis had "far reaching historical significance in encouraging comrades of the whole Party and people of the whole country to emancipate their thinking and follow the correct ideological line."[22] This meant that Mao Zedong Thought was not static and unchanging, but rather flexible: "If everything had to be done according to books and thinking became ossified, progress would become impossible, life itself would stop and the Party and country would perish."[23] Ideology must be appropriate to the historical moment, and be confirmed by practice for it to have meaning. The "Two Whatevers" line, with its rigid adherence to Mao's sayings, would ultimately undermine the historical movement of the Party. Deng had said in 1977 that "If this principle were correct, there could be no justification for my rehabilitation, nor could there be any for the statement that the activities of the masses at Tiananmen Square in 1976 were reasonable."[24] If Hua were right to stress the Two Whatevers, then Deng's version of the the national myth was incoherent and inconsistent.

In addition to the shift in orthodoxy, certain events in the national myth were reevaluated and important verdicts on several key events were reversed. In particular, these events were in relation to Deng and his allies in economic matters. These reversals had to occur if the reform agenda was to be put into place. Rhetorically, the historical accounts had to be reversed, so that the nation might be unified under the leadership of Deng:

> Satisfactory settlement of these questions is very necessary for consolidating stability and unity, facilitating the shift in the focus of the work of the whole party, and getting the whole Party, the whole army and the people of all our nationalities to unite as one.[25]

For example, the session reversed earlier decisions on Deng Xiaoping's heterodoxy, and portrayed Deng as having been intimately involved in the successes of the Party:

> The session points out that in 1975, in the period when Comrade Teng Hsiao-ping [Deng Xiaoping] was entrusted by Comrade Mao Tsetung with the responsibility of presiding over the work of the Central Committee, there were great achievements in all fields of work."[26]

In addition, the document declared that the dismissal of Deng over the April, 1976 Tiananmen rallies was unjust, in that there was nothing "counterrevolutionary" about the rallies:

> The Tian An Men events of April 5, 1976 were entirely revolutionary actions. The great revolutionary mass movement, which unfolded around the Tian An Men events and in which millions upon millions of people in all parts of the country expressed deep mourning for Comrade Chou En-lai and indignantly condemned the gang of four, provided the mass base for our Party's success in smashing the "gang of four."[27]

After the downfall of the gang, the nation had restored correct ideology, and consequently the entire nation was progressing economically:

> The session points out that the restoration and development of our national economy since the downfall of the "gang of four" has been very rapid, and that there have been marked increases in total industrial and agricultural output value and revenue in 1978."[28]

Because of these historical reversals, the Communique began to account for the change in policy direction. By criticizing the history put forth by the Gang of Four and replacing it with an historical account favorable to Deng, the meeting established a new accounting of the national myth that was crucial to the later implementation of the Dengist line.

Several key Party leaders, such as Peng Dehuai and Deng's ally Yang Shangkun, were also rehabilitated. Not only was their revolutionary character reaffirmed, but their orthodoxy was recognized. In addition, the document warned about the dangers the nation faced if a wrong view of history prevailed:

> Only by firmly rejecting false charges, correcting wrong sentences and rehabilitating the victims of frame-ups can the unity of the Party and the people be consolidated and the high prestige of the Party and Comrade Mao Tsetung upheld.[29]

The document's identification of the prestige of the Party with Mao's image was important, in that Mao still served as the key authorizing figure of the Party. Although Mao's policies were being reversed, as well as his version of the national myth, the deceased Mao was referred to as a "great Marxist" and given credit for the revolution:

> Without his leadership and without Mao Tsetung Thought, it is most likely that the Chinese revolution would not have been victorious up to the present. The Chinese people would still be living under the reactionary rule of imperialism, feudalism, and bureaucrat-capitalism and our Party would still be struggling in the dark.[30]

Although none of Mao's mistakes were mentioned in the Communique, intimations of a later reevaluation were mentioned: "It would not be Marxist to demand that a revolutionary leader be free of all shortcomings and errors. It also would not conform to Comrade Mao Tsetung's consistent evaluation of himself."[31] Thus, the plenum slowly began to dismantle the cult of Mao, which portrayed Mao as omnipotent, infallible, and omniscient.

The official response to the Third Plenum illustrated the strategic importance of the meeting to Deng's new influence and power. One media report stated:

After hearing the broadcast of the communique . . . the cadres and masses . . . pledged their support for all major decisions of the plenum on guaranteeing that the country's 800 million people carry out a victorious new Long March, and the plenum's strategic policy decision on shifting the stress of party work and the attention of the people to socialist modernization.[32]

The importance of the meeting for the national myth was also noted. One Party official said that

The political, economic, organizational and theoretical problems solved at the plenum were all matters of fundamental importance concerning the future and destiny of the Party and the country, and it reflected the demand of history and the people's aspirations."[33]

In the official view, then, History itself demanded the verdicts, reflecting the doctrine of historical progression.

The Third Plenum began a rhetorical trajectory that would set China on the long march to economic reform. The initial steps were small but significant: the repudiation of hard-line Maoism as ideological orthodoxy and the attempt to legitimate policies designed to spur economic growth by appealing to Mao's own words. Deng Xiaoping was acknowledged as the new interpreter of ideology, and his interpretations became orthodoxy. The meeting reaffirmed the national myth, while also reversing much of the previous version, those elements that had propped up support for Mao and Hua and denigrated Deng. Mao's personal authority still remained problematic, however, and would not be seriously challenged until the Sixth Plenum of the Eleventh Central Committee in 1981, when the influential *Resolution on CPC History* would be released.

The *Resolution on CPC History* and the Demystification of Mao Zedong Thought

Earlier, I noted that Mao Zedong's charisma at the time of his death was reminiscent of the emperor worship of the dynastic period of China's history. Frederick Wakeman has noted the religious nature of Mao's status:

Chairman Mao, whose benevolence was "higher than the mountains and deeper than the sea" (*shan kao, hai shen*—language once reserved for the Son of Heaven) had become a kind of cosmic savior, no man or god greater than he.[34]

Given the overwhelming importance of Mao's personal charisma, the success of the People's Republic was largely bound up with popular perceptions of Mao, and any aspersion cast on Mao was interpreted as a direct attack on China. Since the common understanding of the Party's history was virtually synonymous with the history of Mao's leadership, it was unthinkable to denigrate Mao entirely. Any attempt to discount Mao's mythic image in the eyes of the peasants who venerated Mao would destroy the epic history of the Communist Party. One scholar of Chinese politics noted in the early 1980s that "Mao and Mao Thought can and must be criticized but cannot and must not be abandoned . . . Indeed, it is far too early to let Mao's reputation die with him."[35]

Deng realized that the legitimacy that Mao's image evoked was crucial to maintaining the credibility of the Party. In a speech to the drafting committee of the 1981 *Resolution on CPC History*, he argued that the very legitimacy of the Party was wrapped up inextricably with Mao's personal authority:

> If we don't mention Mao Zedong Thought and don't make an appropriate evaluation of Comrade Mao's merits and demerits, the old workers will not feel satisfied, nor will the poor and lower-middle peasants of the period of land reform, nor the many cadres who have close ties with them. On no account can we discard the banner of Mao Zedong Thought. To do so would, in fact, be to negate the glorious history of our Party. The appraisal of Comrade Mao Zedong and the exposition of Mao Zedong Thought relate not only to Comrade Mao personally but also to the entire history of our Party and our country. It's not merely a theoretical question that is involved but also and especially a political question of great domestic and international significance.[36]

The credibility of the Party itself was on trial in the public discussions as to Mao and his wisdom. If Mao were shown to be a tyrannical emperor, then the prestige of the entire revolution would crumble. James Myers sums up the problems encountered by an overreliance on Mao for the legitimation of political doctrine:

The new CPC leaders were, however, sensitive to the related issues of doctrine and legitimacy. Mao was way too important; he could not be savaged the way Khruschev had attempted to savage Stalin. Mao was China's Lenin, and as founder his role was too central to the legitimacy of Communist rule in China for him simply to be dismissed as "wrong."[37]

The maintenance of Mao's image was vital, then, if the legitimacy of the Party itself was to be maintained. However, the continued lionization of Mao prevented the implementation of the reform agenda that Deng and the pragmatists had set themselves to accomplish. Meisner notes the constraints placed on the policy decisions that could be implemented as long as Mao's image still dominated Chinese consciousness:

> Also required was the demystification of Mao Tse-tung, whose ghost dominated the political consciousness of the new era almost as much as his person had dominated the political and social life of his own time. The legitimacy of the new regime . . . could be established only by reducing the stature of the Great Helmsman. Maoist policies and ideological precepts could be abandoned, or revised, only by demonstrating the fallibilities of their author.[38]

Similarly, Andrew Nathan has argued that the reformers faced a dilemma, in that they risked their own legitimacy if their debunking of Mao went too far:

> The challenge facing the Deng group was to repudiate all that had been done in Mao's name during the Cultural Revolution without discrediting the monopolistic structure of power that had enabled him to do these things. They had to separate the party from twenty years' deeds of the man who had led it, while leaving the party dictatorship intact.[39]

The leaders of the nation were caught in a dilemma; they needed to "demystify" Mao to move forward with reforms, and yet in so doing they risked undermining their own base of authority. The solution to this dilemma was to distinguish the mythic charismatic image of the chairman from the fallible human behind the image. In other words, the Mao of the national myth had to be retained, while the Mao who had established ideological orthodoxy had to be dismissed. The mythic Mao could then be appropriated as needed, while Mao the theorist could be discredited.

Although some scholars and Party members had begun to indirectly question Mao's legacy immediately after his death, none of these directly attacked Mao.[40] The trial of the Gang of Four also undermined Mao's prestige, as it seemed evident that Mao had a larger role in directing the Gang of Four than was acknowledged. In spite of all the unofficial and veiled criticisms of Mao, it was not until an official pronouncement of Mao's mistakes was offered that the the nation could move away from the ideological constraints provided by Mao.

The official response to Mao was finally provided by the 1981 *Resolution on CPC History*, issued in response to President Ye Jianying's call for a formal summing up of recent Party history; the specific aim of which was to gain the "great objective of building a powerful and modern socialist country" by uniting all citizens and affirming the direction of the Party and the nation.[41] The document released was formally titled *Resolution on Certain Key Questions in the History of Our Party Since the Founding of the People's Republic of China*, or, more informally, the *Resolution on CPC History*. Deng and his supporters saw the document as an opportunity to consolidate their legitimacy by explaining recent Party history and establishing the official direction of the Party.

The *Resolution on CPC History* sought to settle questions about Mao's legacy by redefining ideological orthodoxy and redefining Mao's role in the national myth. The next section of this chapter will discuss how these two objectives were met.

Recreating Mao Zedong

One of the most important contributions of the *Resolution* was its revised historical judgment of Mao Zedong. It transformed Mao's image from a demigod, infallible and omnipotent, to a very human leader, capable of disastrous mistakes. The contributions of Mao to the Chinese revolution were acknowledged, although Mao's authority was gently downgraded by referring to him as but one member in the overall leadership structure. The contributions of other Party members were given more attention and Mao was referred to as the "chief representative" of the Party, rather than its core. By emphasizing the contributions of the Party as a whole, the document established the contributions of other Party members to the progress of the revolution.

Since the *Resolution* is a documentary history of the Party, many other details of the national myth were altered or reversed. Peng Dehuai's fall from favor, as well as Liu Shaoqi's and Deng Xiaoping's, were given full explanations as to why the original verdicts were incorrect. Since the Central Committee seemed to be anxious to document the "70:30" formula, that Mao's policies were 70 percent good and 30 percent bad, the document carefully sifted through the history of the Party to verify exactly what had been good and what had been bad. The document revised the national myth just to the extent that the overall transcendence of the myth was not lost, while many of the supporting details were either reinterpreted or left out altogether.

The harshest criticisms of Mao in the document concerned his role in the Cultural Revolution. Although the Communique of the Third Plenum stated that the Cultural Revolution was a "great revolution," and that it was directed toward good ends, the *Resolution* unequivocally decreed that the decade was one of turmoil and disaster.[42] Not only was the Cultural Revolution wrong, but its ideological basis was declared unorthodox. The *Resolution* specifically insisted that Mao's theoretical errors were in violation of Mao Zedong Thought:

> These erroneous "left" theses, upon which Comrade Mao Zedong based himself . . . were obviously inconsistent with the system of Mao Zedong Thought, which is the integration of the universal principles of Marxism-Leninism with the concrete practice of the Cultural Revolution. These theses must be clearly distinguished from Mao Zedong Thought. The history of the Cultural Revolution has proved that Comrade Mao Zedong's principal theses for initiating this revolution conformed neither to Marxism-Leninism nor to Chinese reality.[43]

The key argument here is that the ideological basis for the Cultural Revolution was inconsistent with the universal, objective truths of Mao Zedong Thought. Mao's teachings were distinguished from Mao Zedong Thought. The document accomplishes the rhetorical task of maintaining the legitimacy of the Party by arguing that Mao Zedong Thought was a crucial part of the revolution, not necessarily Mao Zedong. Mao Zedong Thought was defined to include all "scientific" and "correct" teachings, regardless of who had actually taught them.

Since Mao was merely human, he fell victim to incorrect ideology, and the *Resolution* argued that the Cultural Revolution illustrated the impact of invalid ideology. One scholar has argued that the image of Mao that emerges from the analysis is a "tragic hero."[44] In other words, his personal qualities and dedication to the revolution were heroic, but he was unable to overcome his own hubris. The *Resolution's* conclusions concerning him were that:

> While making serious mistakes, he repeatedly urged the whole Party to study the works of Marx, Engels, and Lenin conscientiously. . . . Herein lies his tragedy. All these important facts are inseparable from the great role played by Comrade Mao Zedong. For these reasons, and particularly for his vital contributions to the cause of the revolution over the years, the Chinese people have always regarded Comrade Mao Zedong as their respected and beloved great leader and teacher.[45]

It is symbolic of Mao's treatment in the *Resolution* that all of the references to him were as "Comrade Mao Zedong," rather than as "Chairman Mao Zedong." The one notable exception to this pattern is in a section that repudiated the erroneous "Two Whatevers" policy of Hua Guofeng. The identification of Mao as "Comrade" emphasized his identification with the people, rather than his distance. The Chinese word for comrade, *tongzhi*, means one with the same heart, the same will, the same aspirations. As Chairman, Mao made terrible mistakes; but as Comrade, his mistakes could be overlooked because of his revolutionary wisdom. As Chairman, he was at times driven by arrogance; as Comrade, Mao was guided by his consubstantiality with the people of China, regardless of his mistakes. As Chairman, Mao perpetuated erroneous theories, but as Comrade, he codified the wisdom of the Party into Mao Zedong Thought. As Chairman, Mao's legacy can be dispensed with, but as Comrade, Mao's legacy and his mythic status are invaluable. And thus, Comrade Mao was honored not as an infallible interpreter of ideology, but as a leader of the people, one whose heart beat with that of his nation.

The *Resolution* stressed the absolute need for understanding that from a fallible human leader had come a set of infallible directions:

It is entirely wrong to try to negate the scientific value of Mao Zedong Thought and to deny its guiding role in our revolution and construction just because Comrade Mao Zedong made mistakes in his later years. And it is likewise entirely wrong to adopt a dogmatic attitude towards the sayings of Comrade Mao Zedong, to regard whatever he said as the immutable truth which must be mechanically applied everywhere . . . Both these attitudes fail to make a distinction between Mao Zedong Thought—a scientific theory formed and tested over a long period of time—and the mistakes Comrade Mao Zedong made in his later years. And it is absolutely necessary that this distinction be made.[46]

The rhetorical nature of this necessity is clear when we consider the importance of ideological orthodoxy to legitimate policy. Deng Xiaoping reportedly had desired to downgrade Mao's image in the Resolution even further, but inner-Party feuding prevented him from doing so. Ultimately, the compromise image of Mao in the document was more consistent with the Mao of the earlier national myth. Since the Party was still relying on Mao Zedong Thought as a scientific basis for progress, any confusion between Mao and Mao Zedong Thought would undermine the legitimacy of the Party. By maintaining the infallibility of Mao Zedong Thought, and retaining for itself the ability to define that Thought, the Party maintained its most valuable asset—ideological certainty.

By downgrading Mao from a god-emperor to a human leader, the *Resolution* enabled the reformers to break away from Mao's directions and policies, while still appropriating the mythic appeal of Mao the revolutionary. The national myth is maintained with what seem to be only minor revisions. However, there was still the matter of Mao's hold on ideology. To break the constraints of Mao's "ultra-leftist policies," the *Resolution* also addressed itself as to the matter of Mao's ideological contributions.

Redefining Ideological Orthodoxy

As mentioned previously, the guiding ideology for the Chinese nation since the 1949 Revolution had been Marxism–Leninism–Mao Zedong Thought. The importance of Mao's teachings to the nation as a basis for ideological orthodoxy cannot be overstated. Helmut Martin argues that Mao's words acquired a "universally valid, almost legislative force."[47] During the height of the cult of Mao during the Cultural Revolution, Mao's thought was elevated to a quasi-supernatural level. By reflecting on Mao's thought, patients could overcome cancer, workers could attain supernatural feats, and doctors could resurrect the dead.[48] On Mao's death, *People's Daily* comforted the nation with the words:

> Chairman Mao has parted with us forever. The great leader and teacher has left us a priceless treasure of revolution—the invincible Mao Tse-tung Thought. The radiance of Mao Tse-tung Thought will forever guide the progress of the Chinese people.[49]

The phrase "Mao Zedong Thought," however, had no clear referent, and could mean many things. Stuart Schram notes that before the *Resolution*, two different definitions of Mao Zedong Thought were in currency.[50] The first definition included what Mao actually thought about, wrote, and said during his long life, while the second definition included the four volumes of Mao's *Selected Works*, his red book, and the policies propagated during the sixties and seventies.[51] The *Resolution*, however, distanced Mao Zedong Thought from Mao himself while redefining it as "Marxism–Leninism applied and developed in China."[52] In other words, Mao Zedong Thought is the correct application of the scientifically derived principles of Marxism-Leninism in the Chinese cultural context, regardless of the origin of the application. This definition of Mao Zedong Thought radically recreated the content of ideological orthodoxy in China, rhetorically creating a vastly different legitimating artifact.

The framers of the document were not willing to allow the powerful rhetorical tool of "Mao Zedong Thought" to remain ambiguous. The *Resolution* established three key principles of Mao Zedong Thought: to seek truth from facts, the mass line, and Chinese independence and self-reliance. By outlining these three principles as the essence of Mao Zedong Thought, the document established Deng Xiaoping's pragmatism as orthodoxy. The first principle, that of seeking truth from facts, means merely that truth must be derived from practice. The document quotes Mao as saying that "correct knowledge can be arrived at and developed only after many repetitions of the process leading from matter to consciousness and then back to matter."[53] In other words, if it works, then it must be true. This principle enshrines as ideological orthodoxy Deng's pragmatism, for which he had often found himself out of favor. Deng's quote from the 1950s that "It doesn't matter if the cat is black or white, as long as it catches mice," rather than being heretical, was shown to be a logical extension of Mao's own thought. In addition, any lingering doubt left over from the 1978 truth debate was swept away, as Deng's understanding of truth was now verified by the scientific Mao Zedong Thought.

The principle of the mass line meant simply that correct ideology can only be derived from the people. I argued in Chapter 2 that much of the mythic appeal of the early Party and revolutionary period was due to Mao's affirmation of the peasantry, and the establishment of the "dictatorship of the proletariat." By reaffirming its commitment to the peasantry, the *Resolution* enshrined this value as a defining characteristic of the Communist Party:

> As the vanguard of the proletariat the Party exists and fights for the interests of the people. But it always constitutes only a small part of the people, so that isolation from the people will render all the Party's struggles and ideals devoid of content as well as impossible of success.[54]

Finally, independence and self-reliance were affirmed as the third principle of Mao Zedong Thought. As noted in Chapter 2, the identity that Mao had helped the nation to forge was a powerful rhetorical force. This nationalism is noted by Jung Chang:

> It was under Mao that China became a power to be reckoned with in the world, and many Chinese stopped feeling ashamed and humiliated at being Chinese . . . he enabled the Chinese to feel great and superior again, by blinding them to the world outside. Nonetheless, national pride was so important to the Chinese that much of the population was genuinely grateful to Mao. . . .[55]

The principle of self reliance meant that China must not rely on other countries' experience of Marxism; rather, it must implement Marxism on its own terms. By reaffirming independence and self-reliance, the *Resolution* reaffirmed the nation's dignity, as well as the national myth.

One rhetorical function that this reconstitution of Mao Zedong Thought provided was maintaining the weight of ideological orthodoxy, while introducing flexibility. Whereas Hua Guofeng had committed himself to Mao's policies by allegiance to the Two Whatevers principle, the reformers were able to implement policies unconstrained by previous commitments. Both relied on the authority of Mao Zedong Thought, but the *Resolution*'s version was ambiguous enough to allow for different policies.

A second benefit of this looser construction is that the decisions and policies of other revolutionary leaders could be enshrined as contributing to Mao Zedong Thought. Since Mao Zedong Thought was the correct implementation of Marxist principles, and was not exclusive to Mao, the policies of more moderate members of the Party, such as Zhou Enlai and Liu Shaoqi, could be identified as contributions to Mao Zedong Thought and used to legitimate present policies. The new construction allowed the Party to recreate what Mao Zedong Thought was, rather than assume that there was a static core to it.[56]

A third rhetorical function provided by this new delineation of Mao's thought was the reaffirmation of the basic values that brought about the initial attraction of the nation to the Party. Chinese intellectuals were attracted to the Communist Party largely because of its commitment to national independence and self-reliance. Peasants were attracted by the early land reform policies and Mao's emphasis on the mass line. By reaffirming the virtuous ideology of the Party, the mythic heroism and integrity of the Party was maintained among all of the major constituencies of the nation.

The *Resolution*'s greatest rhetorical significance, then, was to reconstitute Mao's mythic image into a more manageable form, and to redefine ideological orthodoxy, thus freeing the leadership from the ideological constraints of strict Maoism. By deflating Mao Zedong's charismatic image, the legitimacy of the Party he had led for four decades was maintained, and transferred to the very person Mao himself had removed from power twice before, Deng Xiaoping. By reconstructing Mao Zedong Thought, innovative policies could be implemented, needing only to meet the three principles set forth.

Although the *Resolution on CPC History* affirmed the epochal shift to socialist modernization begun by the Third Plenum, the legitimation of the economic reforms was still not settled. Just because Mao had now been downgraded did not mean that the reform agenda was automatically affirmed. The next section of this chapter will examine the manner in which the Twelfth Party

Congress in 1982 continued the rhetorical trajectory of the reform movement by identifying economic modernization as the very heart of Mao Zedong Thought.

The Twelfth Party Congress: Renewal of the Correct Line

After the victories of the Third Plenum and the publication and approval of the *Resolution on CPC History*, the eventual establishment of the economic direction seemed secure. Maoist leaders were systematically removed from high positions, and the economic reforms were welcomed by large segments of the nation, particularly those whose standards of living increased. Preparations began for the Twelfth Party Congress to be held in September of 1982.

In one sense, then, the direction of the nation seemed secure. Deng Xiaoping was firmly in control of the Party apparatus, and the ideological battles with Hua Guofeng had subsided, with Hua the clear loser. At the opening of the Twelfth Party Congress, Hua had been assigned the most junior position on the rostrum, and his errors were firmly written into Party history. However, the rhetorical dismantling of Mao's legacy, as well as the quick pace of structural elements of the reforms led to a new set of distinct problems.

First, there was an increased skepticism toward Marxism and the Marxist vision in China. Intellectuals, who had historically supported the Party's efforts, began to question whether the Marxist vision was merely chimeric, and to call for more open political structures and processes. It seemed to some that the move to demystify Mao might actually overwhelm the Party, as many throughout the nation had personal grievances against the Party, especially those in the intellectual class.

Second, the reform movement was resisted by some who were unsatisfied with the quick turnaround in policy and the minimizing of Mao's legacy. Many saw real tangible benefits for continuance of previous policies. Included within this group were military commanders with real political power as well as Party hardliners who had risen to power during the Cultural Revolution.

The 1982 Twelfth Party Congress, which Deng dubbed the most important Congress since the Eighth Party Congress in 1956, was a crucial event in reinforcing the overall thrust of the government's direction after 1978. Structurally and organizationally, the

Congress's most important functions were to further purge the Party of "leftist" elements, verify the economic directions of the nation, and strengthen Party discipline and membership through the release of a new Party Constitution.

Rhetorically, however, the Congress had to strike a middle ground between those who called for more radical change and those who feared the directions taken by the reformers. Deng and his reformist colleagues sought to bridge this division by reaffirming the national myth as presented in the *Resolution on CPC History* and reaffirming the dominance of Marxist ideology. The headline of an article about the Congress in the *Far Eastern Economic Review*, entitled "How history was revised: Hua reviled, Hu revived," captured the spirit of the Congress and illustrates the direct historical appeal advanced at the Congress.[57] In fact, the documents released from the Congress strengthened the Party's claims to legitimacy by portraying the Party as a victim of the personality cult of Mao. The Congress validated the legitimacy of the reforms by focusing on two broad areas of restoration: the restoration of the correct line of the early Party, before the creation of the cult of Mao, and the restoration of the mythic dimensions of the Party itself by reestablishing ideological unity and orthodoxy. Together, these two broad pushes validated the reforms and the continued leadership of the Chinese Communist Party, two goals that had become increasingly confused and conflicted in the minds of many citizens.

Deng Xiaoping made a brief speech at the Congress in which he verified its historical importance. He claimed that the Party was following the correct line articulated at the Eighth Party Congress in 1956, but not implemented because of the ideological incompetence of many in the Party. The present Congress would restore the correct ideological line that had been subverted by the personality cult of Mao as well as the scheming of those who had set themselves up against the Party. Deng's goal was clear, to again revise the national myth by arguing that the correct ideological line had been subverted well before the 1966 opening of the Cultural Revolution, but actually as early as 1957 by Mao's insistence on the Great Leap Forward. With this argument, two decades of Communist party error could be swept away, maintaining as a part of the national myth only the Civil War period, roughly from 1921 to 1949, and the first seven years of Communist party rule, from 1949 to 1956.

The goal of this historical revision was to demonstrate the importance of building a "socialism with Chinese characteristics."

By acknowledging the two decades of error, from 1957 to 1978, the Party was able to purify its reputation and lead the nation into utopia, a powerful, modern, and socialist China:

> In carrying out our modernization programme, we must proceed from the realities in China . . . To integrate the universal truth of Marxism with the concrete realities of China, blaze a path of our own and build socialism with Chinese characteristics—this is the basic conclusion we have reached in summing up long, historical experience.[58]

Deng's emphasis upon making Marxism conform to China was not new in Chinese history. Even Mao, as early as 1938, had argued for the "sinification" of Marxism, perhaps in an attempt to resist the dominance of the Soviet Union.[59] Documents from the 1978 Third Plenum noted the necessity of combining the "universal truths of Marxism with the concrete practice of socialist modernization," but did not draw substantive conclusions regarding China's unique experiences. Deng Xiaoping's reintroduction of the concept, therefore, is rhetorically significant, as it became the basis for the later theoretical justification of the reforms, in creating the theoretical space to introduce new elements to the Chinese economy.

In spite of Deng's introduction of the phrase into the national vocabulary at the 1982 Congress, it was not a key part of Hu Yaobang's major report. It would achieve greater prominence later, when in 1984, the Party released many of Deng's writings and speeches in a book entitled *Building Socialism with Chinese Characteristics*.[60] Hu Yaobang's speech at the Congress, however, helped to lay the groundwork for later theoretical innovation by arguing that the appropriate goal of the nation as early as 1956 was economic modernization.

Hu's address at the Congress, entitled "Create a New Situation in All Fields of Socialist Modernization," sought to reclaim the legitimacy of the early Party and argue that the 1978 Third Plenum had restored ideological orthodoxy. Although his speech was not meant to be a historical documentary, as was the *Resolution on CPC History*, its further revision of the national myth was important for the legitimation of nonorthodox economic measures. The premise of Hu's argument was that legitimacy of the early Party was based on its struggles with and for the peasants, as well as its ideological purity. This early confidence the nation had in the Party, however, had come under question because of the ideological heterodoxy that had crept in through the devices of people such as the Gang of Four and Lin Biao. Hu argued further that since the 1978 Third Plenum, the Party had corrected itself, therefore restoring its moral authority.

Hu revisited the mythic history of the Party established in the *Resolution* to provide historical grounding for the Congress and the reforms. Given the doctrine of historical progression, it was important not to be seen as in any sense "backing up," or reversing historical trends. To accomplish this, it was necessary that he recount the national myth and demonstrate exactly where the nation had gone astray and the necessary correctives.

Hu argued that the early Party had all of the courage and zeal necessary to lead the nation. During times of heavy military losses, the Party had demonstrated its sufficiency:

> The Party was not overwhelmed by the enormous difficulties. Under the leadership of a number of outstanding figures of whom Comrade Mao Zedong was representative, the party displayed rare revolutionary courage and fortitude, fought on tenaciously, strove creatively to find a revolutionary path suited to China's specific conditions and turned the tide, resuscitating the revolutionary cause and bringing about a new situation of victorious advance.[61]

After the completion of the revolution, though, the Party had gone astray, largely because of theoretical error and the development of the cult of Mao. Once heterodoxy became established as orthodoxy, the Party's authority was undermined. Hu's speech earnestly documented the destructive power of "leftist" mistakes. "Leftist" errors were those that proceeded from not taking into account the objective situation, while "rightist" errors were those that attempted to somehow restore capitalism. Reversing the previous insistence of the Party that "rightist" mistakes were more damaging to the cause of national progress, he noted the responsibility of Hua Guofeng for allowing leftist mistakes to persist:

> During the two years before the Third Plenary Session of the Eleventh Central Committee, the question of rights and wrongs in the Party's guiding ideology was not clarified as it should have been and the work of setting things to rights proceeded haltingly.[sic][62]

In spite of the fact that the Eleventh Party Congress in 1976 had declared an end to the Cultural Revolution, Hu argued that the ideology that had undergirded the Cultural Revolution had not been renounced. However, at the 1978 Plenum, this error had been corrected:

> In the sphere of ideology, we have resolutely broken the fetters of dogmatism and the personality cult which existed for a long time, and have reaffirmed the Marxist ideological line of seeking truth from facts, thus infusing a dynamic and creative spirit into all fields of endeavor. We have restored the original features of Mao Zedong Thought and persisted in and developed it under new historical conditions.[63]

In other words, Mao Zedong Thought had been systematized and molded into a more manageable form, one that was more sympathetic to actual development. Mao Zedong Thought, therefore, was now more trustworthy. Moreover, since the 1978 Third Plenum, the Party had remolded itself into the body it had once been. "It (the Party) has done much to rectify Party style, gradually revived its fine traditions, and become more mature and firmer in the course of struggle."[64] By eliminating bad ideology and bad decision-making styles, the Party had prepared itself for further historic advances.

Because of this restoration of the Party in both ideology and style, the Party was well-equipped to lead the nation through the "new situation" of economic and technological modernization. The most important of the changes facing the nation was economic modernization. However, the policies of reform and openness would never violate the fundamental principles of the socialist movement, including the preeminence of public ownership and the leading role of the planned economy.

Hu's speech did not just stress the readjustment of the correct ideological line. In response to a deepening mistrust of the Party, as well as the Marxist view of history, he called for a reaffirmation of the Communist Chinese vision, or the eschatological vision of history. Specifically, he called for the development of a "socialist spiritual civilization," a term initially introduced by Ye Jianying in 1979 and later developed by Deng Xiaoping, but receiving its most authoritative treatment in Hu's speech.[65] "Socialist spiritual civilization," in Hu's usage, refers to the complex of ideology, values, and morality of Marxism, which serve the all-crucial goal of prodding the forces of history toward their final fulfillment. Ideology, and its accompanying morality, is vital not only in establishing the development of economic structures and material civilization, but ensures the "correct" orientation of that development.

Hu argued that the emphasis on "spiritual civilization" was necessary because of assaults on two fronts: the view that Communism is but a "dim illusion," or a disenchantment with the true faith; and the corruption that comes from exposure to "spiritual pollution" from outside; specifically, the West.[66] Thus, the spiritual civilization of the early days of the Party had been damaged by the ideological damage done by the Gang of Four, the Cultural Revolution, and Mao's personality cult, as well as by the attraction to the bourgeois cultures sweeping into China from the West. The campaign for a "spiritual civilization" served two functions; to shore up the original commitment to Marxism, and to serve as a warning to the young not to engage in distasteful or questionable political activities.[67]

Hu's emphasis on a "socialist spiritual civilization" was a direct analogy to early Confucian teachings on virtue. Just as the Mandate of Heaven was dependent on a virtuous ruler, so correct ideology is dependent on a "socialist spiritual civilization." Only by guaranteeing the moral and ideological correctness of the Party members would the Party be assured of having a continuing role in world history. Without socialist spiritual civilization, the nation was in danger from internal collapse. With this emphasis, then, ideological orthodoxy is reaffirmed as having a central role in the legitimacy of the Party:

> Ideological education in the Party is the pillar of the building of spiritual civilization in the whole society, and Party members should, first of all, play an exemplary role morally and ideologically . . . We must not allow our policies or work in any field to impede or, still worse, to undermine the building of a socialist spiritual civilization.[68]

Only by making sure that all Party members shared the same ideological understanding, morality, and energy could the Party maintain its mythic, historical role as the "vanguard of the proletariat." This goal was advanced by the release at the Congress of the new Party Constitution, which in effect, strengthened the requirements of membership, and provided means by which slack or undisciplined members could be more easily released from Party membership.

Hu reminded the Congress that "History has entrusted our Party with heavy responsibilities in the great undertaking of China's socialist modernization."[69] The agency that Hu attributes to the impersonal forces of history is forcefully reminiscent of the agency of Heaven on behalf of past emperors. In the Chinese national myth, though, such agency is necessary, for it is the agency of History that delivers the Mandate, and hence, the legitimacy of the governors.

The Twelfth Party Congress, then, rhetorically shored up the reputation of the Party as the sole legitimate leadership structure in the nation, as well as the ideological foundations of the nation. By reaffirming the role of the Party in history, the national myth was again called on as a testimony to the legitimacy of the government, quelling the dissent of agitators who secretly or not so secretly wished for the dissolution or overthrow of the Party. By stressing the ideological work necessary to attain a high level of "socialist spiritual civilization," the Congress not only appeased the hard line elements unsettled by the pace of the rebuilding of the economic structures, but also demonstrated the clear resolve of the leadership not to tolerate unorthodox ideas.

The Congress was designed not just to clarify the ideology and the present tasks, but to persuade the nation that the path was correct. The rhetorical force of the Congress was well understood by Hu, who declared that:

> The principles and tasks to be defined by this Congress will enrich and develop the correct line followed since the Third Plenary Session . . . Richer in content and closer to reality, they will be even more persuasive in unifying the thinking of the entire Party and the people of all our nationalities and become an even more accurate guide to our action.[70]

The Congress reaffirmed two key legitimating principles, the importance of the Party in history and the importance of ideology. In other words, the Congress affirmed both the mythic view of historical progression, and the role of the Communist Party in that progression, as well as the required virtue to maintain the mandate:

> The historical experience of the Party . . . teaches us that the fundamental reason why the Party has been able to lead the

Chinese people in winning one great victory after another is its integration of the universal truth of Marxism with the concrete practice of the Chinese revolution.[71]

Only the Party could lead the nation in modernization, and the Party could only attempt such a feat when armed with the correct ideology, the ideology of modernization and reform.

When viewed from hindsight, it is possible to trace the beginning of a "rhetorical trajectory" of the legitimation of the economic reforms. The Third Plenum relied heavily on grounding the reforms in Mao's own policies and directions. The 1981 *Resolution on CPC History* began the official deconstruction of Mao's legacy and created a "more perfect" Mao. Finally, the 1982 Twelfth Party Congress again relied on a historical recounting to argue that the legitimacy of the Party should not be based on Mao's authority as a "demigod," but on his contributions, as well as the contributions of others, to the early period of the revolution. By restoring the Party's line and its morality, the Party prepared itself to lead China into a new stage of historical development.

All of the documents discussed relied heavily on the rhetorical power of the national myth. By retelling the mythic history of the nation, the documents attempted to appropriate the legacy of the early revolutionary Party. In addition, these retellings created some stunning reversals of historical verdicts, such as the cases of Peng Dehuai, Liu Shaoqi, and, most important, Deng Xiaoping. Whereas earlier versions of the myth portrayed these early revolutionaries as "capitalist-roaders" or "counterrevolutionaries," the new version depicted them as loyal, courageous, and heroic patriots who suffered because of their willingness to stand against the cult of Mao. The basic story line of the national myth, however, was unchanged.

The appropriation of the national myth was important for another reason, and that is that the doctrine of historical progression was retained and applied to the "new situation" in China, that of economic modernization. The documents and speeches argued that China had come to a new phase, and that the tasks of the Party must therefore change. The doctrines and dream of revolution were not doubted, but the Party argued that previous policies were no longer relevant. Much as dynastic changes were regarded as reflecting the eternal purposes of the Mandate of Heaven in imperial China, the changing emphasis from class struggle to economic modernization was portrayed as reflecting the eternal progression of history.

Rhetorically, then, the documents put forth very much the same argument as new dynastic rulers would, that the change in regime was due to external forces.

The importance of ideological consensus and orthodoxy was also carefully reaffirmed within these documents. The reformers, no less than Mao, saw ideological consensus and education as crucial to China's continued prosperity and unity. Rather than relying on a single corpus of texts, however, the reformers put forth a new criterion for truth that eventually became enshrined as Mao Zedong Thought. This perspective maintained that pragmatism was the correct ideology. This meant that socialism was defined as that which worked the best. Although the infallibility of ideology was never questioned, the subtle alteration of the dominant orthodoxy allowed unprecedented movement away from the policies of Mao Zedong.

In spite of the careful reconstruction of history and reliance on ideological orthodoxy, however, the reforms continued to bog down and the people of China were unwilling to accept the Party's view of history. The easy answers provided by the new version of the myth, that China's chaos was due mostly to the intrigues and conspiracies of the Gang of Four, were largely insufficient. The Cultural Revolution, in particular, remained a sticking point for a great number of Chinese. It was clear to many that their personal turmoil was due not to the machinations of the Gang of Four but rather to the pettiness and greed of local level Party members. As one worker who had been persecuted in the sixties argued:

> What's the use of dwelling on it? Now we're called on to look forward into the future, aren't we? Blame everything on the Gang of Four. Bury the horrors of the past. Too many people suffered and nobody wants to talk about it. But I figure our sufferings can't just be written off, right?[72]

As long as these grievances remained, and those who prospered from the Cultural Revolution remained in power, the grassroots legitimacy of the Party would be subject to criticism. The excesses of China's campaigns contributed to an unwillingness to believe anything too much.

In addition, the new ideology, although welcomed by entrepreneurs and peasants, was too vague to provide the kind of unity that the government had hoped for. By opening the discussion on the problems with strict Maoism, the Party had in a real sense opened a Pandora's box of criticism. Dissent became more outspoken, and China's intellectuals in particular were unwilling to just make more money. The impact of the Beijing Democracy Wall movement and the accompanying underground publications went far beyond the immediate surroundings, as intellectuals throughout the nation openly questioned China's future.

There also seemed to be unresolved questions related to the absoluteness of ideology. The reformers did not seem to recognize the incoherence in ascribing theoretical and ideological mastery to Mao, and naming the reigning orthodoxy after him, while still affirming that the theoretical and ideological errors he made caused the devastation of the Cultural Revolution. Finally, the scientific pragmatism that was enshrined as orthodoxy established no clear parameters for orthodoxy. Influences from the West became particularly bothersome to many Party stalwarts who began to worry for the future of the Party.

The early attempts at legitimating the reforms helped to reestablish China's ideological consensus. The chains that had bound Hua Guofeng were finally broken, and China was able to move forward in its trek toward modernization. In Chapter 4, I discuss the impact of the reforms in the mid-1980s and demonstrate how the Thirteenth Party Congress not only legitimated the reforms, but made them mandatory.

4 The Thirteenth Party Congress and "The Primary Stage of Socialism"

The early stages of economic reform in China garnered support around the world for Deng and his allies. The Western world in particular applauded Deng and his allies for introducing the reforms, and some even speculated that China had abandoned Marxism altogether. William Safire, for example, wrote that the biggest event of 1984 was the Chinese Communist Party's "embrace of capitalism."[1] Deng was twice honored as *Time* Magazine's Man of the Year, in 1978 and 1985, and some analysts declared that the reforms would be reliable models for the rest of the Communist world to follow.[2] Even Mikhail Gorbachev's government in the Soviet Union looked to China as a model for reform.[3]

Although Deng and the reformers garnered praise abroad, they did not enjoy universal acclaim at home. Even though the reforms seemed legally and practically entrenched, and the reformers held control of the major institutions, criticism of government policies came from both the right and the left. Hard-line conservative leaders, many of whom had been displaced by the reformers, complained about the intrusion of negative influences from the West. In contrast, many citizens, particularly students, clamored for more far-reaching reforms of the political system. Economic problems, such as dissatisfaction with arbitrary pricing structures and a growing income gap between workers and peasants, also contributed to the choruses of criticism.

In Chapter 3 I argued that the Third Plenum of the Eleventh Central Committee and the Twelfth Party Congress reversed the policies of Mao's final two decades, while still preserving the legitimacy of the Chinese Communist Party. At the 1978 Third Plenum, the work of the Party was shifted from class struggle toward economic development. The reformers relied on Mao's prestige in the national myth to justify this shift. The Twelfth Congress similarly grounded the reforms in the early revolutionary legitimacy of the Party and attempted to demythologize Mao's vision by declaring the late 1950s the original point of departure from ideological orthodoxy. In the attempt to distance China from Mao's ideology, however, they inadvertently created an ideological vacuum. After Mao's vision of the past was repudiated, it was perhaps only natural to also question his vision of the future.

As the reforms became increasingly distanced from their Marxist moorings, the early rhetorical justifications for the reforms began to weaken. The Chinese leadership used the Thirteenth Party Congress in 1987 to shore up this weakening legitimacy by providing a broad mandate for further economic restructuring. By introducing the theoretical innovation of the "primary stage of socialism" (*shehui zhuyi de chuji jieduan*), the Party redefined the existing ideological basis for China's economic system and provided a mandate for greater reform.

While the primary stage doctrine provided an ideological justification for continuing and strengthening the reforms, it failed to provide a compelling national mythic history that preserved the legitimacy of the Communist Party. There are three goals to this chapter: to describe the increasing ideological confusion in Chinese society during the mid-1980s; to examine the rhetorical impact of the 1987 Thirteenth Party Congress in reformulating ideological orthodoxy while maintaining the vision of the national myth put forth at the Twelfth Party Congress; and finally, to describe the persuasive power of this new rhetorical justification for the continuation of the reforms.

The Stagnation of the Reform Drive

By 1984, the reforms had solidly taken root throughout Chinese economic structures. Agricultural production surged and industries continued to restructure to achieve maximum production. However, as the Thirteenth Party Congress approached, the reform drive began to falter because of pressing concerns over economic inequity, the political challenges mounted by students and intellectuals, and the ideological challenges to the reforms by the more conservative Party elders. These political and economic consequences created a perception that the reforms were benefiting only the privileged from elite backgrounds. To borrow from Jürgen Habermas's analytical scheme, the expectations of the populace for a better standard of living went unfulfilled, precipitating a legitimation crisis.

By 1985 the negative side of economic growth had become more apparent, as an overheated economy and surging inflation caused popular resentment toward the rising inequities between geographic areas as well as social groups.[4] Critics of the reforms were able to undermine the credibility of the program merely by juxtaposing official propaganda promoting the newly rich against China's traditional commitment to egalitarian socialism. The favoritism shown to the new special economic zones and urban areas precipitated more wealth for residents of these zones, raising the ire of those in rural or backward areas. Since much of the new wealth was brought in by, and taken out by, foreigners, some criticized the policies as a new form of economic imperialism, functionally equivalent to nineteenth-century military and political imperialism.

Corruption by officials taking advantage of the reforms also raised popular resentment. High-profile cases, such as a foreign exchange scam on Hainan Island involving the loss of U.S.$1 billion, as well as numerous local cases of officials using their connections to obtain goods not openly available, seemed to prove the claim that the reforms were only good for causing greater crime and corruption. Increasingly, public attention focused on cases of corruption among high-ranking Party members and their children, the so-called princelings. As the children of elites had more access to power and resources, they also had more opportunity to take advantage of their privileges for material benefits.

Besides these economic and social pressures generated by the reforms, the reform agenda was also slowed by ideological questions as to the nature of the program, leading to what one analyst called a "theoretical morass."[5] Without a solid theoretical grounding, the reform program seemed only to generate ambiguity about what was politically acceptable and what was not, thus producing more anxiety and hindering the implementation of the reforms.[6]

John Burns and Stanley Rosen argue that although there was general consensus among the Party leadership as to the direction of the reforms, at least four areas of debate provoked controversy: (1) the appropriate methods for achieving modernization, (2) the likely consequences of rapid modernization for the Party in the state and the society, (3) the nature of governing structures in the changed economic situation, and (4) the lessons to be gained from the experience of three and a half decades of Marxism.[7] While the first three are primarily ideological in nature, the last speaks directly to the heart of the national mythic history.

It was inevitable that these questions would surface among the citizenry, given the important shifts in social and economic life. For the top Party leadership, these questions were even more pressing. The more radical reformers, such as Zhao Ziyang, called for a more rapid reform program, one that would give greater latitude to private ownership, market mechanisms, and economic inequality. Others, such as Deng's old ally Chen Yun, favored more limited reforms, and remained skeptical of the orthodoxy of the reforms. In the early stages of the reforms, these divisions were effectively masked. By about 1985, however, when the last remaining Maoists were retired from office and the reforms began to have a greater impact, the differences between the two groups became more pronounced.[8] Eventually, it seemed that the more radical reformers were advocating policies that would replace central planning in the economy altogether, in favor of market mechanisms. This group also sought to deflect criticism by arguing that the economic problems the nation faced were not due to the reforms themselves, but to the constraints placed on the reforms by an overreliance on traditional Marxist values.

To the conservatives, it seemed that the radical reformers were calling for the replacement of socialism by Western capitalism. Conservatives questioned what the terms "socialism" and "capitalism" meant, since it was obvious that the reformers had radically altered their official meanings. In addition, popular criticism of traditional culture and values, which the reformers had seemed to advocate, threatened not only Marxism, but Chinese self-reliance and nationalism as well.

Party members also became increasingly concerned with the perceived breakdown of political harmony. Although most in the Party agreed that some relaxation of ideological constraints was necessary, few were prepared for the widespread social unrest fostered by economic and ideological relaxation. At the end of 1986, for example, Chinese students launched demonstrations throughout the nation to demand more freedom and democracy, under the rule of science. To many of the Party faithful, especially those who had suffered during the catastrophic decade of the Cultural Revolution, these demonstrations were nothing less than anarchy, and could only be responded to by quick and decisive force. Jonathan Spence has argued:

> The last thing that Deng or other veterans of the Cultural Revolution wanted was a new wave of youthful violence that would pit one wing of an uncontrollable mass movement against another, leaving the CCP fractured and impotent in the middle. They had already seen where that could lead.[9]

To the students and intellectuals, the reforms had substance only if they were accompanied by far reaching legal and political changes. Although the students were encouraged by the early changes, they were uncertain of the future. Spence argues that "it was slowly becoming clear that millions of Chinese . . . found it difficult to get their bearings in China's shifting landscape or to see where they were going."[10] The ambiguity of the leadership toward issues such as political and legal reform illustrated the uncertainty regarding China's future.

The Party leadership sought to check the trend toward open criticism of the Party quickly by launching campaigns against "spiritual pollution" and "bourgeois liberalization." Two prominent intellectuals, astrophysicist Fang Lizhi and journalist Liu Binyan, were purged from the Party because of their alleged influence over the students and attacks on the Party. Fang had become an important inspiration to the students because of his open advocacy of democracy and his attempts to restructure the prestigious university he presided over in line with his political commitments. Liu, who had gained fame by his muckraking exposés of corruption, was seen as a hero of true socialism because of his courage in reporting corruption among Party leaders.

The questioning of orthodoxy was unsettling to Party elders who had suffered during the Cultural Revolution. As Lucian Pye argues, there seems to exist in the Chinese political system a profound fear of chaos or disorder among the political elders that leads them to place an overwhelming emphasis on ideological consensus.[11] To many in the Party, then, these events seemed to indicate that the social and political costs of the reforms outweighed any economic benefit to be gained from them. Many began to question if the economy was really in need of such radical medicine.

Hu Qiaomu, Mao's former secretary, voiced in 1980 a warning that seemed relevent: "Our society is not like a park [like Hyde Park], where everyone can voice his opinion and when everything is finished no harm has been done, no flowers have been injured, and everyone leaves the park and goes home."[12] Although Hu no longer held a government post, many others in the Party and government seemed to share Hu's concern over the social trends. One Party stalwart, upset by the students' questioning of the Party's legitimacy, lashed out:

> The Chinese Communist Party is a great, glorious and politically correct party that has always retained its revolutionary vigor. The leadership of the Communist Party is not granted by heaven, but by countless revolutionary martyrs who, wave after wave, shed blood and sacrificed themselves for half a century.[13]

As the time drew near for the Thirteenth Party Congress in October of 1987, the legitimacy of the reform agenda was in serious straits. The orthodox national myth was openly questioned by important segments of society, as students and intellectuals directed challenges to the very heart of revolutionary legitimacy. The unifying ideology, when not openly questioned, became muddled as relentless power struggles were waged between ideological factions. The clear vision of China's past, present, and future was replaced by imprecise predictions and the fear of future Party clashes.

The Thirteenth Party Congress: Revision of Myth and Ideology

As the Thirteenth Party Congress opened in October of 1987, it was clear that a new mandate was essential to justify the reforms in the face of challenges to the Party and the new economic inequities. Zhao Ziyang clearly stated this compelling mandate:

> The central task of the current Congress is to accelerate and deepen the reform . . . We shall analyze our experience, uphold

and develop the line followed since the Third Plenary Session, . . . define the basic policies for future economic development, economic structural reform, and political structural reform, and decide on basic principles for strengthening Party building as we carry out reform and the open policy. By fulfilling these tasks correctly we shall do much to promote unity within the Party and between the Party and our people of all nationalities, and to ensure our continued advance along the road of socialism with Chinese characteristics.[14]

A new mandate was also needed for the continued leadership of the Communist Party under the authority of Marxism. Twenty out of the thirty-eight years since the founding of the People's Republic were now publicly acknowledged as having been a disaster. The Party had to argue that regardless of the past, it was still the only legitimate leadership structure. The mythic role of the Party as China's savior had to be preserved. To accomplish this, Zhao Ziyang's keynote speech attempted to distance the policies of the present Party leadership from the policies of the past leadership. Zhao located a moment of historical turning at the Third Plenum of 1978:

It should be said that in the last nine years (since the Third Plenum) the national economic strength has increased more rapidly and the people have obtained greater material benefits than in any other period since the founding of the People's Republic. This is in sharp contrast to the situation in the period of 20 years from the late 1950s to December 1978 . . . During those years, under the influence of the 'Left' guiding ideology, 'class struggle' was taken as the 'key link,' economic development met frequent setbacks and the people's standard of living improved only slightly.[15]

This is in direct contrast to the earlier justifications, which attempted to demonstrate the essential unity of the reforms with the early Party, and requires a radical rethinking of the guiding ideology and the national myth. The way in which the Party chose to meet the ideological demand was to insert a new historical stage into the national myth, the stage of the "primary stage of socialism." By inserting a new stage into the evolutionary progression of communism, the Party altered the traditional way of understanding the national myth and added a compelling historical mandate for the reforms.

Simply stated, the new doctrine asserted that the full implementation of socialism was to be accomplished through distinct stages, and that each stage was to be accompanied by certain policies. None of the stages could be skipped or altered, because certain historical processes had to occur at each stage. Marx had certainly taught similar things before, and although the concept of an early stage of socialism had been introduced to the Chinese before, it was not fully developed until the Thirteenth Congress.[16]

According to Zhao's development of the doctrine, China is a socialist nation, but one only in the beginning stages of socialism. Thus, China had emerged from a semifeudal, semicolonial state to socialism, but not an advanced socialism. Because China had never really gone through a stage of capitalism, especially advanced capitalism, the means of production had not been fully developed, thus leaving China with few productive industrial resources.

Because of this, the nation had been unable to overcome the poverty that characterized feudalism. Since the productive forces lagged behind, true socialism could not be implemented. Socialist development could only occur after the productive forces had been fully developed. The iron law of history dictated as such. However, that was not to say that China should reorient itself around a capitalist vision:

> Under the specific historical conditions of contemporary China, to believe that the Chinese people cannot take the socialist road without going through the stage of fully developed capitalism is to take a mechanistic position on the question of the development of the revolution, and that is the major cognitive root of Right mistakes. On the other hand, to believe that it is possible to jump over the primary stage of socialism, in which the productive forces are to be highly developed, is to take a utopian position on this question, and that is the major cognitive root of 'Left' mistakes.[17]

A correct understanding of China's situation, then, dictated that China should allow the productive forces to develop in the primary stage of socialism, thus necessitating some capitalistic measures. Without this intermediate phase, China was doomed to remain in poverty.

Zhao argued that the primary stage of socialism was not a stage common to all nations, but rather one particular to China, because of China's unique history of having attempted to "jump over" the capitalist stage. The experiences of other nations were not adequate as models for China, nor could China's experience be considered the norm for other nations. This argument freed China from the constraints of "international communism," as no transitional experience could be considered a guide for China:

> Building socialism in a big, backward Eastern country like China is something new in the history of the development of Marxism. We are not in the situation envisaged by the founders of Marxism, in which socialism is built on the basis of highly developed capitalism, nor are we in exactly the same situation as other socialist countries. So we cannot blindly follow what the books say, nor can we mechanically imitate the examples of other countries. Rather, proceeding from China's actual conditions and integrating the basic principles of Marxism with those conditions, we must find a way to build socialism with Chinese characteristics through practice.[18]

This argument clearly contradicted Mao's assertion decades earlier that since China was undeveloped, it remained a "blank slate" on which anything at all could be written. Mao believed that since there were no developed means of production and accompanying economic structures, China had none of the characteristics of advanced capitalism to overcome, and thus was at an advantage over other socialist nations. Zhao's argument that this was a disadvantage clearly contradicted Mao's vision.

Zhao also clearly distinguished between the primary stage of socialism and the transitional stage from capitalism to socialism. The transitional stage was completed in the early 1950s when public ownership of the means of production was established. The primary stage also differed from the final stage of Marxism, a "stage in which socialist modernization will have been achieved." This process would take at least one hundred years from the transitional period, or until about 2050.

The reason for the clear demarcation of these periods becomes more evident by reference to the national myth of the revolution. It would be inconsistent with the national myth to argue that the leaders had led China into socialism before the nation was ready, as the

Comintern had suggested during the early days of the Chinese revolution. To say so would be to undermine the epic history of the revolution, and also imply that socialism was inappropriate for China. Rather, by arguing that there were distinct stages in the implementation of socialism, the legitimacy of the early policies of the Communist Party was upheld.

Since early policies, such as the nationalization of private industry, were reversed by the reforms, it seemed that these policies were being repudiated in favor of capitalism. If a clear distinction between the stages were not made, it would only lead to questions as to why private industries were nationalized in the first place. By arguing that the stages are different, and that each stage has its own historical goals and purposes, and hence policies, then the reforms are not seen as contradictory to the early policies, only as fulfilling a different historical function. It was right to nationalize industries in the fifties, and it is right to denationalize them in the eighties. With this distinction, then, the mythic status of the Communist Party was not compromised. The legitimacy of the CCP, and its early policies, was maintained.

In like manner, the vision of the "socialist modernization" stage, which presumably still referred to the advanced communist era, was maintained in the eschatological framework of the Party. By clearly demarcating a different historical phase for the current reforms, the policies are not seen to undermine the eventual goal, a fully communist nation. Just as feudalism was more advanced than a "natural" economy, and yet still inferior to later developments, so the primary stage can be portrayed as superior to the "semifeudal, semicolonial" state, while still inferior to advanced socialist modernization. Any advancement marks progress, and the advantages to be gained during the primary stage are not to be neglected just because they will no longer be in place in the final economic and social stages.

Since the primary stage of socialism would last at least one hundred years from the time of the initial transition into socialism, the Chinese nation would have until around 2050 to implement the reforms and build up China's productive forces. In establishing a definite time period for the primary stage, Zhao was attempting to stave off criticism of the reforms for another half a century. Since the primary stage would not be completed for so long, it was still too early to critique the policies.

Zhao further subdivided the primary stage into three steps, marked by the relative affluence of the people, and beginning at the

Third Plenum of 1978. The first step would be the doubling of the 1980 GNP, the second the redoubling of the economy by 2000, and the third, to be accomplished by the middle of the next century, would see the per capita GNP equivalent to that of moderately developed countries. Zhao claimed that the first goal had been obtained, and the task of the present Congress was to see the second accomplished.

It was not only the national myth that was altered by the introduction of the primary stage doctrine. Ideological orthodoxy was itself affected. Zhao's speech attempted to provide a revised orthodoxy by appealing to the material progress the reforms had brought about. Since truth is affirmed and validated in practice, the practice of the reforms validated the theoretical and ideological orthodoxy of the doctrine. In vibrant language of liberation and victory, reminiscent of Mao's language of victory over class struggle, imperialism, and colonialism, Zhao argued that the pragmatic gains made during the reform movement illustrated the correct nature of the reforms. Such a claim could not have been made before Deng's victory in the "practice is the sole criterion of truth" debate at the Third Plenum:

> Reform and the open policy have broken down the rigid economic structure and revitalized the economy. The socialist commodity economy has grown vigorously and with irresistible momentum . . . The enthusiasm of the masses has been brought into play, and this has further liberated the productive forces. Reform and the open policy have also further emancipated the minds of the people, battering down many old concepts that have long stifled their thinking. It is becoming a trend for people to seek change, to blaze new trails and to stress practical results.[19]

He argued that the material progress of the previous few years resulted from emancipation from both the "ossified thinking" of reform critics and the "bourgeois liberalization" of dissidents. Those who did not come to the same conclusions were obviously ideologically incorrect; however, this would not quench the enthusiasm of the masses for change:

> Bourgeois liberalization still has appeal for some people, and ossified thinking still shackles some comrades' minds. Above

all, comrades throughout the Party and the people as a whole are strongly dissatisfied with the bureaucratism and corruption that exist to varying degrees in many sectors.[20]

Zhao argued that the reforms were necessary for China to achieve its rightful place in the world, and so fulfill the national myth. In addition, history itself mandated the reform process, much as during the dynastic period, the old Mandate of Heaven determined who should rule China. Economic and technological concerns, the new mandate, would define the future. If China did not continue the reforms, historical progression would be undermined:

> If we do not recognize this and redouble our efforts, our country and our people fall further behind, and China will not be able to take its rightful place in the world. History requires our generation and the next few generations . . . to rouse themselves, unite as one, and do all they can to catch up.[21]

In addition to establishing economic progress as the fundamental goal of history—and therefore, the Party and the nation—Zhao also asserted that Deng Xiaoping was China's foremost theoretician. Deng's role in establishing the reform agenda was gratefully acknowledged, and he was made the hero of the new historical era. The new line, and thus the new era, bear Deng's imprint most strongly:

> Comrades! Nine years' practice has proved that our Party is truly a great glorious and correct party and that the line followed since the Third Plenary Session of the Eleventh Central Committee is a correct, Marxist line. This line is a crystallization of the wisdom of the Party and the people, and of the collective wisdom of the Central Committee. With his courage in developing Marxist theory, his realistic approach, his rich experience and his foresight and sagacity, Comrade Deng Xiaoping has made significant contributions to the formulation and development of this line, to decision-making on a series of key issues, and to the creation of a new situation in construction, reform and opening to the outside world.[22]

Thus, Zhao attempted to assuage fears of a rampant capitalism by assuring the Party that the reforms were Marxist in their orientation. In addition, he argued that a more thorough understanding of Marxism would enable them to understand China's actual predicament, in the primary stage of socialism.

Aware that he was introducing a theoretical innovation, Zhao attempted to answer in advance any questions as to why no one had recognized the different stages before. In particular, why had Mao Zedong, heralded during his time as the world's greatest Marxist, not been aware of the primary stage of socialism? Zhao was able to explain Mao's oversight by attributing it to Mao's theory of contradictions. Mao's theory, following Lenin, posited that contradiction, or conflict, is endemic to human life. The key conflict of each historical era, however, varies.[23] Since the primary contradiction changes through different historical periods, the means of resolution of the contradictions also differ.

Careful not to reject Mao's theory of contradiction altogether, Zhao (following Deng) argued that the period of contradiction based on class was largely over, and that the principal contradiction of the present stage is between the growing material and cultural needs of the people on the one hand, and backward production on the other. Since this was the primary contradiction of the present historical era, then all efforts of the CCP are to be directed toward resolving this conflict, and all means that helped to accomplish this goal were essentially Marxist–Leninist.

Zhao argued that Mao had misunderstood this, because he had taught that the primary contradiction of the era was class struggle, thus limiting the potential for economic growth. Following Mao, the Party had allowed many incorrect policies to be put into place:

> Many things which fettered the growth of the productive forces and which were not inherently socialist, or were applicable only under certain particular historical conditions, were regarded as 'socialist principles' to be adhered to. Conversely, many things which, under socialist conditions, were favourable to the growth of the productive forces and to the commercialization, socialization and modernization of production were dubbed 'restoration of capitalism' to be opposed. As a consequence, a structure of ownership evolved in which undue emphasis was placed on a single form of ownership, and a rigid economic structure took shape, along with a corresponding political structure based on overconcentration of power.[24]

In other words, an incorrect understanding of the primary contradiction had led to inappropriate policies, much as if a doctor's misdiagnosis would lead to wrong medicine. Policies that were entirely appropriate for one historical era were evaluated on the basis of criteria that applied to a different era.

Once Zhao had established that the primary contradiction was one of economic growth, then the correct and appropriate resolutions could be broached:

> To resolve the principle contradiction of the present stage we must vigorously expand the commodity economy, raise labour productivity, gradually achieve the modernization of industry, agriculture, national defence, and science and technology and, to this end, reform such aspects of the relations of production and of the superstructure as are incompatible with the growth of the productive forces.[25]

Zhao went on to establish several principles that should guide this transformation, including policies concentrating on modernization, persisting in comprehensive reform, adhering to the policy of openness to the outside world, and developing a planned commodity economy with public ownership playing the dominant role. The Four Modernizations, of agriculture, defense, science and technology, and industry, would be the goal, while the Four Cardinal Principles—keeping to the socialist road, upholding the "people's democratic dictatorship," leadership by the Communist Party, and Marxism–Leninism–Mao Zedong Thought—would be the guide. These principles are summed up in the "one center, two basic points" formula; that the one central goal of the nation is to develop the productive forces, and the two basic points are to uphold the Four Cardinal Principles and to persevere in reform and the policy of openness to the outside world.

Although reform policies would certainly lead to a restructuring of the economy, the planned economy would remain paramount: "The socialist economy is a planned commodity economy based on public ownership."[26] The control and security of the centrally directed economy would not be forsaken, regardless of the growth of the private economy. With this pronouncement, Zhao probably meant to assuage the fears of many conservative Party members who foresaw an overthrow of the planned economy.

Although careful not to give too much hope to the democracy movement, Zhao argued that a restructuring of the economy necessitated the reform of the political structures as well. It was only through reformation that China's socialist system would prove its superiority to the capitalist societies of the West:

> The purpose of reforming both the political and economic structures is, under the leadership of the Party and the socialist system, to better develop the productive forces and to take full advantage of the superiority of socialism. In other words, we shall catch up with the developed capitalist countries economically and politically, we shall create a democracy that is of a higher level and more effective than the democracy of those countries.[27]

Democracy as envisioned by the West was not what Zhao had in mind, however. Rather, Zhao meant by democratization the withdrawal of the party from administrative tasks better suited to the government. Zhao still strongly affirmed the traditional Chinese characteristic of a powerful central authority under the ideological certainty of Marxism:

> The system of the people's congresses, the system of multiparty cooperation and political consultation under the leadership of the Communist Party, and the principle of democratic centralism are the characteristics and advantages of our system. We shall never abandon them and introduce a Western system of separation of the three powers and of different parties ruling the country in turn.[28]

The goals of political reform were to eliminate bureaucratism and the overconcentration of power. The specific solution to this problem was to make a distinction between the functions of the Party and the state. These actions would not lower the Party's standing, but instead raise it: "It must be pointed out that when there is no distinction between Party and government, the Party's position is in fact lowered and its leadership weakened."[29] By getting involved in administrative work, the Party compromised its position as the cutting edge of the proletariat. Specifically, the corruption that emerged on the part of Party members had brought disrepute to the Party, and only by separating itself from government and state functions could the Party fulfill its historic role in leading the nation.

At the close of his address, Zhao reiterated the need to uphold the ideological system on which China was based. The scientific accuracy of Marxism–Leninism–Mao Zedong Thought was not to be questioned, as it provided the very foundation on which China was built:

> Socialism with Chinese characteristics is the product of the integration of the fundamental tenets of Marxism with the modernization drive in China and is scientific socialism rooted in the realities of present-day China. It provides the ideological basis that serves to unite all the Party comrades and all the people in their thinking and their action. It is the great banner guiding our cause forward.[30]

Having said this, however, Zhao was also quick to point out that Marxism was not a static ideology, but one that required critical analysis and revision: "Marxism is a science that keeps developing in practice. In the contemporary world it is generally recognized that Marxism needs further extensive development."[31] Only by rejecting dogmatism and rigid applications of Marxism could the superiority of Marxism be shown. Thus, Zhao reaffirmed the importance of Marxist ideology for China's national purposes, preserving the legitimating power of scientific Marxism.

Zhao also attempted to strengthen the visionary components of China's revolution. He reaffirmed the causes for which Mao labored, nationalism and socialism, and added to these an important third goal, that of modernization:

> China's revolution and development represent an important component of the progressive cause of mankind. The founding of the People's Republic of China, which shook the world, has strengthened the progressive forces of the world and expanded the influence of Marxism. With the success of its socialist modernization, China will unquestionably make a new contribution to world peace and to the progress of mankind and further increase the appeal of scientific socialism. Having triumphantly taken the first step towards the grand objective of socialist modernization, we shall work hard to take the second and third steps and win greater victories. We are convinced that the road of socialism with Chinese characteristics will become wider and wider.[32]

The impact of this broadening of the national myth is profound. The enemies of the Communist Party, over whom victories were to be won, are no longer the forces of imperialism and colonialism and bourgeois capitalism, but rather, the forces of stagnation and poverty. The primary contradiction was not class oppression, but the contradiction between development and poverty. The utopian goal of the national vision was no longer just the existence of a classless society, led by the proletariat and measured by the degree of egalitarianism, but a modern society, led by technologists and managers and measured by a per capita gross national product. The epic struggle of revolution was maintained; populated not by heroic warriors, but by technologists and entrepreneurs. Liberation was not from class enemies, but rather from poverty and backwardness.

The Persuasive Power of the Primary Stage Doctrine

Reception to the doctrine in China after the Congress was varied. One analyst observed that the introduction of the theory was generally demoralizing, since it implied that after three decades of Communist rule, the nation was still only in the primary stage of socialism. Others argued that the theory represented a step backwards to a regressive capitalism, and still others believed that the standard of socialism itself had been lowered, to include elements, such as markets, profit motives, and stocks, that Marx had considered exploitive.[33]

To the Party leadership, however, the Congress and its doctrine was a huge success. Official publications hailed the establishment of a new basic blueprint for China's future and development.[34] The leadership praised the continuance of the line from the Third Plenum, and claimed that the Congress "made a more refined and systematic exposition on the theory of the primary stage of socialism in our country."[35] Overseas commentators argued that factional differences among the leadership seemed to have disappeared at the Congress.[36] The Hong Kong journalist Lam Wo-lap declared that the Congress broke new ground for the entire socialist world by legitimizing Adam Smith's "invisible hand" theory.[37] One Western diplomat argued that Zhao had "staked out an awesomely large terrain for economic reform. And future arguments will be over how or when—and not whether—reform will be carried out."[38]

The Thirteenth Party Congress attempted to address the concerns of all critics by subtly revising the national myth put forth at earlier Party meetings and the 1981 *Resolution*, and arguing that the primary stage doctrine legitimated the introduction of market-oriented reforms. To appease the students and dissidents, Zhao reaffirmed the scientific nature of the reforms, and continued to stress that pragmatic concerns were the sole criterion of truth. He argued that the material progress of the previous nine years was proof of the legitimacy of the Party, demonstrating that the Party could indeed deliver material progress. In addition, Zhao reaffirmed the need for political reform, which meant the elimination of corruption.

To conservative critics of the reforms, Zhao argued that the reforms in no way undermined the nation's Marxist moorings. Rather, the doctrine of historical progression, which any true Marxist would affirm, mandated the reforms. By arguing that China was only in the primary stage of socialism, Zhao created ideological space for the reforms.

The theory of the primary stage of socialism rhetorically accomplishes several important tasks. First, it explains and excuses the poverty still existent in China after almost four decades of rule by the Communist Party. The poverty was not due to Communist rule, but rather due to the historical situation. The Communist Party could not be expected to change historical progression itself, it could only guide the nation through the historical stages that in themselves are immutable.

Second, the theory further freed China from the ideological constraints on policy that had become increasingly burdensome to the implementation of the reforms. The reforms had been subject to at least four constraining forces; the writings of the original Marxist theorists; the implementation of Marxism in other nations, such as the Soviet Union; the early policies of the Communist Party itself; and finally, the eschatological vision of a Marxist utopia. By arguing that the primary stage of socialism called for different policies from both earlier and later stages, the theory freed China from each of these constraints.

In effect, the doctrine inserted a new historical stage into an ideology built on historical stages, a stage in which all the policies of the other stages were anachronistic. The historical drama itself is never questioned; rather, it is strongly reaffirmed. But the presence of the new stage makes the critiques placed on it seem out of place; the critiques don't apply because they are drawn from a different historical epoch.

Thus, the primary stage doctrine rewrites history in at least two senses. One, it rewrites the absolute and scientific Marxist his-

tory that dictates the movement of human society to include elements previously unimaginable. Without rewriting the beginning
and the closing chapters, the middle chapters are written in a way
that best seems to capture the period, with little fear of inconsistency. Much as a novel could be constantly revised in the middle as
long as it begins and ends the same way, the reforms can take any
form whatsoever as long as they end at communism. The inevitability of a new stage in Chinese history makes the policies appropriate
to that stage acceptable.

Two, it rewrites recent Chinese history by establishing a
revised framework by which that history is to be evaluated. China's
history is not to be evaluated on the basis of progress in class struggle, campaigns, or egalitarianism, but rather on its economic
progress. The rhetorical impact of this assessment is enormous, and
establishes, in effect, a complete rethinking of Chinese history. For
example, the doctrine asserts that Mao's understanding of his own
historical period was erroneous. Since Mao misread his own epoch
and claimed that class struggle was the key link, Mao himself was
responsible for the wasted twenty years from late 1950s to the 1978
Third Plenum. The agreed-on 70:30 ratio for evaluating Mao's
legacy—that 70 percent of Mao's accomplishments were good and
30 percent bad, had to be reconsidered if the conclusions of the Thirteenth Party Congress were taken seriously. Although this ratio
might be valid numerically, the impact of ideological errors, as
opposed to organizational or political errors, would render it invalid.

The 1987 meeting made a stronger pronouncement of the
"new era" in Chinese history, clearly demarcating 1978 as the "era of
Deng Xiaoping." In addition, the national myth was altered by
enshrining economic progress as the goal of history, rather than class
struggle. The early history of the revolution thus is altered, as the
initial stages of liberation from landlords and oppressors are defined
as being only a small element of the ultimate goal, economic prosperity. Thus, China had not completely "stood up" in 1949, but had
merely shaken off some of its remaining feudal shackles and gotten
off its knees. The realization of the true Chinese Communist state
would occur when China had achieved its position as a nation of
wealth and international influence.

This particular alteration of the national myth accomplishes
the goals of justifying the changes under Deng Xiaoping, but ultimately risks undermining the authority of the Communist Party.
Since China was now perceived to be in a different historical epoch,

what then was the value of the continued leadership of the Party? In fact, the Party came to be seen by many as but a way station on the road to prosperity. Many would acknowledge that it took the Party to restore China's dignity, but would argue that since that stage was now over, the Party should quietly depart from the stage of history.

On the other side of the tension of legitimation, though, was the introduction of a new theoretical paradigm that would establish the Marxist credentials of the reforms. In this sense, the primary stage doctrine served as a limited rationale for the reform movement. Since both past and future policies did not necessarily correspond to the present, loyal Party members and citizens could engage in commerce without fear of either reprisal or ideological inconsistency.

However, severe criticisms were leveled against the primary stage doctrine that revealed the fragile legitimacy of the theoretical credentials of the doctrine. Inconsistencies in the theory were apparent to careful observers. For example, Taiwanese critic Ma Feng-hwa argued that Zhao asserted that it is possible to enter socialism without ever going through fully developed capitalism, but that historical inevitability prevents bypassing the primary stage of socialism.[39] It is logically inconsistent to argue that one stage can be inevitable while another can be avoided in a system built on historical inevitability.

In addition, Ma questioned whether a stage that is particular to China, as Zhao asserts the primary stage is, can be historically inevitable. Without theoretical generalizability, can anything be inevitable? Another seeming inconsistency in the doctrine is that the relative strength of private ownership vis-à-vis public ownership seems to undercut the Party's insistence on the predominance of public ownership. If private ownership is acknowledged to be more efficient than public, then how can the nation realistically deliberately weaken the more efficient and productive economic arrangement?

These logical inconsistencies within the doctrine contributed to its limited effectiveness in establishing a firm foundation for China's continued modernization, and probably account for the fact that the doctrine quickly fell into disuse, seemingly disappearing for several years.[40] Although the reform process itself quickened after the Thirteenth Party Congress, its critics on both the left and the right were unassuaged. Students and intellectuals continued to question the legitimacy of Party leadership, and Party conservatives continued to question the chaos that the reform process had initiated. In Chapter 5, I examine the role of the Fourteenth Party Congress in the wake of the expanded reform program and the events of Tiananmen Square.

5 The Fourteenth Party Congress and the Transition to a "Socialist Market Economy"

I argued in Chapter 4 that the objective of the Party leadership at the Thirteenth Party Congress in 1987 was to create theoretical space for the reform program. To achieve this end, the Congress introduced the doctrine of the primary stage of socialism, which mandated the development of productive forces through some forms of capitalistic enterprise. In addition, the Congress offered a revision of the national myth to both conciliate this theoretical innovation with orthodoxy as well as to legitimate continued Party rule. In spite of the innovative "primary stage doctrine," many questions remained unresolved after the Thirteenth Congress. Intellectuals and students, sometimes referred to as the new "rightists," accepted the legitimacy of the reforms, but questioned the continuing ability of the CCP to lead the nation in far-reaching reforms. Conversely, those on the left did not question the leadership of the Party, but they continued to question the legitimacy of the reforms. To appease this element within the government and Party, the reformers had to reaffirm their commitment to the principles of Marxist political centralization and communism. To do so, however, meant that criticisms of Party rule would only grow louder, as reformers, including the intellectuals, called for more political openness.

Both groups raised legitimate questions as to the relationship between the Party and the reforms. How could a Communist Party move further and further away from Marxism and continue to be Marxist? As Roderick Macfarquhar has noted,

> [T]he crux of the Chinese political argument has been over whether or not there is a 'contradiction' between Deng's two basic points: Will economic change solidify or pervert Party leadership and other Communist political values?[1]

Either the Party was legitimate, or the reforms were legitimate, but it seemed inconsistent to argue that both could be so. This tension between "right" and "left" was exacerbated by continual warring in the media over which was the greater error, "rightist mistakes" or "leftist" mistakes.[2] That this debate even took place is extraordinary, as it was conventionally assumed that rightist errors were a greater evil, and those accused of rightism often found themselves either in prison or as a target for criticism.

After the Thirteenth Party Congress in 1987, therefore, the CCP was forced to continue its search for ways to justify both the continuance of the reforms and the legitimacy of the Party. By the Fourteenth Party Congress in 1992, however, a new theoretical paradigm had been devised, designed to both release China from the centralism of its past and of Marxist orthodoxy. The way in which the Party chose to do this was to argue that the bureaucratic centralism that often characterized socialist nations was not endemic to orthodox Marxism. We will examine this theoretical innovation after a brief discussion of the continued crisis of legitimacy after the Thirteenth Party Congress.

Challenges to the Reforms and Party Rule

Immediately after the Thirteenth Congress, the Chinese nation faced at least three major theoretical tensions precipitated by domestic and international pressures. First, the reforms led to overheated economic growth, which created hyperinflation and material shortages painful for many segments of the population. Second, the "downfall" of socialism in Eastern Europe and the Soviet Union diminished the credibility of Marxism as a governing ideology—it refuted its "scientific" nature, and thus contributed to an ever-increasing dissatisfaction among China's intellectuals over the nation's commitment to a discredited ideology. These two tensions contributed to create yet one more, a clear demand on the part of students for political openness that reached its zenith in the 1989 Tiananmen Demonstrations. We will turn to each of these in order.

Critics of the reform program did not have to look far to find practical and theoretical evidence of economic problems. For example, at the end of 1988, the industrial growth had risen at a rate of over 20 percent, resulting in a shortage of raw materials and a mad scramble for resources by self-serving localities.[3] Personal income grew, making consumer demand greater than production, creating severe shortages. In addition, the rapid expansion of disposable income contributed to surging inflation, with rates hovering around 30 percent annually.

The overheated economy was felt not only at the national level, in balance sheets and deficits, but at the individual level, as new consumers continued to try to cushion inflationary losses by excessive consumption.[4] A series of droughts and floods, affecting at least half of the nation's agricultural regions, contributed to a fear of further inflation on the part of the farmers and peasants who had benefited the most from the reforms.[5] While farmers and some workers profited greatly from the reforms, other segments of the population noticed little change in either their living conditions or ability to buy consumer goods. Notable among the have-nots were the intellectuals, who were among the last to receive tangible economic benefits from the reforms. Yan Jiaqi, a prominent dissident intellectual, argued that the introduction of market mechanisms was the main cause of the chaos in the economic reforms. Since only a relatively few well-connected people had opportunity to participate in the private economy, inflation and corruption increased conspicuously.[6] The intellectuals argued that the solution to the inequities was to accelerate the reforms by allowing more widespread participation, and included a call to include political openness as part of the reform program.

The economic chaos accentuated the need to either deeply increase the rate of reform and free up prices or slow down the pace of reform in order to reduce inflation. The political will was not in place to eliminate price control completely, however, and so the only policy open to the leadership was retrenchment. These policies were initially presented at a series of meetings in late 1988 at Beidaihe, a seaside resort for the Party and state elites. Zhao Ziyang argued that a quick price reform process would eliminate much of the inequities, but his arguments were rebuffed in favor of more conservative policies. Zhao's political failure here led some analysts to speculate on the impending downfall of Zhao.[7]

Although Zhao remained in office, it was clear that his quick reform agenda was in trouble. Eventually, even Zhao was forced to support centralized economic decisions to reassert control over the economy.[8] The official explanation for the retrenchment was that as soon as the economy was straightened out, the reforms would again be pursued with vigor. A large number of liberal cadres and intellectuals, however, feared that the momentum for reform was lost, and retrenchment was but another name for reversal.

There was, however, some continued experimentation. In the early 1990s, stock markets opened in Shanghai and the southern city of Shenzhen. The opening of the stock markets precipitated even greater concern on the part of the leftists about the fate of the nation; riots broke out in August of 1992 in Shenzhen because of accusations of official corruption. Party officials expected that there would be a tremendous demand for the opportunity to buy stocks, so they devised a lottery system. Individuals would purchase a lottery ticket, and winners would be able to purchase the stocks. Over one million people had gathered in Shenzhen to participate, and when administrators ran out of the the lottery forms, the streets were overrun with angry investors accusing the administrators of corruption. The rioters overturned police cars and attacked government property, leading many conservatives to argue that the markets were responsible and call for a temporary closing of the markets, if not their complete abolition. The Shenzhen riots were but another example of the chaos that would result from further reforms, and illustrated the dangers of creeping capitalism.

Besides the practical questions as to the beneficence of the reforms, challenges to the legitimacy of the Party and the reforms were intensified as a consequence of international circumstances. The virtual abandonment of Marxism by much of the formerly Communist world also led to an intensification of ideological battles. In response to the fall of Communist regimes, intellectuals questioned the legitimacy of Marxism as the state ideology and the Chinese Communist Party as the rulers of the nation. The leadership was thus forced to rejustify the role of the Party and renew its commitment to Marxist principles. Conservatives, however, argued that the Eastern European nations served as negative examples of the consequences of abandoning orthodox Marxism.

The example of the Soviet Union provided ammunition for both sides. During the late 1980s, China's reform program was widely seen as an example for the Soviet Union to follow, and Soviet visitors routinely visited China and wrote glowing reports about the direction of the reforms.[9] Since China and the Soviet Union had often been at odds over which nation had a "truer" Marxism, this seemed to be a welcome vindication of the Chinese leadership. As the Soviet Union quickly bypassed a conservative reform path in favor of more radical reforms, however, the tension reappeared. China's leadership was cautious in its evaluations of the Soviet reforms. For example, in April of 1990, Premier Li Peng somewhat tentatively declared the Soviets' policy of *perestroika* as socialistic, despite signs that the Soviet Union was moving in unorthodox directions. Li argued, however, that China would not pursue a similar course:

> Each society has its own reality, its own situation, and each has reached a certain stage of development . . . How socialism should develop is a question each should answer for itself . . . We do not have one model for everyone to follow.[10]

This commitment to nationalistic pluralism had its limits, however, for the radical processes of *perestroika* and *glasnost* were accompanied by the undoing of Soviet Marxism, and eventually led to the breakup of the Soviet Union. In a move that undoubtedly shocked the Chinese leadership, Boris Yeltsin declared the Communist Party illegal in Russia. This move struck at the very heart of China's national myth, as the new Russian state created doubts not only about historical progression, but about the role of the Communist Party as the vanguard of history. These turnarounds caused many Chinese, especially the intellectuals, to question whether China's commitment to socialism was progressive or not. The Russian example demonstrated to reformers the necessity of abandoning an anachronistic commitment to Marxism, while it demonstrated to conservatives the danger of introducing reforms at all.

While intellectuals applauded Russia's move, conservatives in China feared going the direction of greater reform, and argued that the Soviet example proved that reforms ought to be dismantled before chaos ensued. Premier Li Peng, representative of the latter group, addressed the concerns of those who feared roaming off the socialist path in 1990. He asserted that "diverse forces . . . are realigning and regrouping, . . . thus bringing greater unrest and turbulence to the world."[11] China would avoid the fate of Eastern Europe, however, by increased diligence in ideological education and training. Li Peng's assurances, however, were not sufficient to convince this group that the CCP was not in jeopardy. One Party-commissioned survey revealed that only 7 percent of university students in Beijing thought that communism was a worthy ideal in 1987, dropping to 6 percent the following year.[12]

Fears of the downfall of socialism were exacerbated by open media discussions as to the benefits of capitalism. In a surprising article published in the influential paper *Guangming Ribao*, or "Enlightenment Daily," one column argued that capitalist nations were far advanced in most areas of modernization.[13] Although it dutifully reminded the reader that historical progression dictated that socialism would eventually replace capitalism, the article was surprisingly honest in listing the advantages capitalist nations held over socialist nations, such as the development of the productive forces and economic efficiency, and prophesied the continued dominance of the capitalist nations over the world economy, at least in the short term. The publication of this article, just one month before the Party Congress, was indicative of the difficulties China's leaders were having in explaining China's continuing poverty.

The theoretical problems facing the reformers were serious in themselves, and seemed to slow the initiative of the reforms. This slowdown soon paled, however, in comparison to the threat posed by the Tiananmen demonstrations, which had a tremendous domestic and international impact on China. The actual number of deaths, officially around 300, pales in significance to the numbers of people who had died during mass campaigns initiated by the left, such as the antirightist movement and the Cultural Revolution. Even if the dissidents were correct in their estimate of 3,000 deaths, this number could not compare to the millions estimated persecuted and killed during the Cultural Revolution. The impact of these relatively small numbers, however, was compounded by the drama of the events and by the extensive coverage given them by the foreign press. The demonstrations threatened to undermine the prestige and legitimacy of the Communist Party in a way unprecedented in New China, and many feared that this would cause the political system to unravel altogether. To illustrate the challenges to the government caused by the demonstrations and the subsequent military takeover of the square, a more extensive discussion of the events of the spring of 1989 is necessary.

Tiananmen Square and the National Myth

Liu Binyan notes that the year 1989 was an unusual year in China, in that the convergence of three major anniversaries seemed to emphasize the real cultural and social poverty that held the nation:

> There were three major anniversaries: the two hundredth anniversary of the French Revolution, the seventieth anniversary of the May Fourth Movement, and the fortieth anniversary of the founding of the People's Republic of China. The relationship among these three anniversaries also stirred emotions. Why has China still not achieved the ideals advocated by the French Revolution—freedom, equality, and fraternity—goals announced by the United Nations Human Rights Manifesto? In the seventy years since the May Fourth Movement, the Chinese have sacrificed so much. Why then have the Chinese people not only failed to achieve more democracy, but been subjected to autocratic rule in the name of revolution? Democratic trends over the world, especially those within the Soviet Union and in many countries of Eastern Europe, were all prompting Chinese intellectuals to take action.[14]

Thus, Chinese intellectuals in the spring of 1989 were deeply concerned with democracy, continued reform of both the political and economic realms, and human rights. These concerns transformed into action on the death of ex–Party Secretary Hu Yaobang. On April 15, 1989, Hu died of a heart attack in Beijing. To the younger generation of Chinese, Hu represented a more moderate and humane form of socialism, partly because he had overseen the process of rehabilitation of those who had been persecuted during the Cultural Revolution, and partly because he had been dismissed from his offices in response to his sympathy for the 1986–1987 student demonstrations. Because of this symbolic role, the Beijing students felt a special sympathy for Hu and began to gather in public groups to commemorate his death. Their sympathy for Hu became the lightning rod for political activism. As Yan Jiaqi notes, Hu's death "became the fuse that ignited the discontent of the people."[15] Students from Beijing University, one of China's most elite schools, led a parade from the campus to Tiananmen Square. In a drama reminiscent of the 1976 Qing Ming demonstrations after Zhou Enlai's death, the public mourning turned to huge demonstrations in support of accelerated political reform.

Although most of the students proclaimed their loyalty to China and the CCP, and argued that they only advocated the rule of science and democracy, conservative leaders in the government perceived a tremendous challenge in the demonstrations.[16] Indeed, at times, challenges to Party rule were direct. For example, one popular slogan was "Those who should have died live, those who should have lived have died," a not-so-veiled reference to the students' wish that Hu should have lived, while Premier Li Peng and Deng Xiaoping should have died.[17] These slogans were interpreted, perhaps correctly, as political arguments that the socialism of Hu should have prevailed, while the iron-fisted socialism of Li and Deng should have died. Slogans eventually became even more explicit, as the students grew frustrated with Party officials' refusal to meet with student representatives.

The demonstrations finally turned to full-blown protests, and the students grew bolder as they discovered their ability to paralyze the city. Hunger strikers in Tiananmen Square aroused the sympathies of people throughout the nation, and the citizens of Beijing protected the students from the police and soldiers. Martial law was declared, but it was completely ineffective. Governmental leaders grew frustrated with the inability of the police and the People's Liberation Army to restore order, and it seemed as if the government and the Party were powerless.

When the demonstrations are viewed from the perspective of the national myth, it is clear that the demonstrations did pose a serious threat to the legitimacy of the Party. The official history that established the mythic qualities of the Party was challenged, to be replaced with an alternate history, one that portrayed the nation as under the tyranny of a corrupt Party. One poster that was placed in Beijing illustrates some students' complete disillusionment with the national myth:

> The history of the Chinese Communist Party positively informs us that it indeed deserves to be called the most evil party of its time. It only cares about its own position and pays

no heed to the future of the country and the people . . . All the promises it made upon founding the country turned out to be nothing more than lies . . . Other than wasting China's youth for forty years, the Communist Party has brought nothing to China . . . Today, the Communist Party, especially its members who are government cadres, has already become a new privileged class of Chinese society . . . Of course, actual power is in the hands of Deng Xiaoping and his relatives, disciples, sycophants, and card buddies . . . Great turmoil across the whole of China is imminent. The Communist Party's day of reckoning is about to arrive. . . .[18]

The CCP was not only found deficient, it was considered absolutely evil. The Beijing students signaled that they were no longer content to wait for the gradual improvement of democratic conditions; they were ready to seize democracy. Conservatives within the government were further shocked by the creation and enshrinement of the Goddess of Democracy Statue in Tiananmen Square, obviously modeled after the Statue of Liberty. It symbolized to the conservatives a rejection of Chinese dignity in favor of an idolatry of all things Western. More important, the statue clearly implied that China was not yet democratic, a claim rejected by the Party. Some participants even went so far as to try to deface Mao's portrait that hung over Tiananmen Gate itself, attacking not only Mao, but also the Party he led and the political system he founded. Although other students caught the vandals and turned them over to the authorities, the vandalism itself was too severe of an indictment for conservatives to overlook.

Throughout April and May, the demonstrations continued to choke Tiananmen Square. Students were joined in their protests by workers, journalists, and citizens from all walks of life. An official state visit by Mikhail Gorbachev scheduled for mid-May was disrupted, damaging governmental credibility. Gorbachev's visit had brought to China hundreds of foreign journalists, who subsequently broadcast the students' demands to the attention of the entire world. While the students were thrilled with all of the attention and the drama of their cause, the Party leaders saw this as a humiliating spectacle. This humiliation demanded an immediate, forceful response.

Within the government itself, there was controversy about the nature of the movement. Zhao Ziyang, for instance, argued that the

students were only calling on the Party to live up to its responsibilities, while President Yang Shangkun charged that Zhao himself had
stirred up the students to gain a political edge.[19] Western reporters
characterized the movement as arising from dissatisfaction with
years of communism, while some members of the Chinese government insisted that the movement was "counterrevolutionary" in
nature, and led by criminals and foreigners.[20] The process of defining
the exact nature of the movement was of crucial significance for
everyone involved. According to the national myth, if the movement was counterrevolutionary and based on foreign intrusion, the
government had every right to take whatever steps were necessary to
quell the rebellion. If the movement represented the actual aspirations of the people, however, the Communist Party had to support it,
or risk losing its legitimacy.

During and after the demonstration, wide-scale propaganda
campaigns from both the Party and the students sought to shape
the public perception of the movement.[21] As evidence for the contention that the movement was counterrevolutionary, the government publicized incidents of corruption among the student leaders
and tried to connect the students with Taiwanese "spies." Deng
Xiaoping told military commanders that the situation developed
into a "counterrevolutionary rebellion:"

> In reality, the opposing side is not only a mass of people who
> exchange truth for lies. It also consists of a group of people
> who have created an opposition faction, and many dregs of
> society. They want to subvert our country and subvert our
> Party: this is the [true] nature of the problem.[22]

The students' counternarratives portrayed the movement as
revolutionary, and themselves as the new heroes of the Chinese
national myth. As I argued in Chapter 2, the May Fourth Movement
of 1919 is enshrined in the national myth as a courageous movement opposing colonialism and the humiliation of China at the
hands of foreign powers. The May Fourth movement is clearly an
iconic symbol of the role of students in bringing about positive social
change. The students clearly saw themselves as the inheritors of
the tradition of student activism and influence, and more important, saw themselves as legitimate agents of social change. The students even went so far in this identification as to draft a "New May
Fourth Manifesto," which stated in part:

Seventy years ago today, a large group of illustrious students assembled in front of Tiananmen, and a new chapter in the history of China was opened . . . Today, in front of the symbol of the Chinese nation, Tiananmen, we can proudly proclaim to all the people in our nation that we are worthy of the pioneers of seventy years ago.[23]

Not only did the students portray themselves as revolutionary, many also sought to demonize the Party and the Army. On June 3, when the government's intentions to use force to clear the square became obvious, and just hours before the actual military encounter, the students released a statement meant to galvanize the resolve of all involved in the demonstrations and to completely shatter the official version of the national myth:

Today is the third of June, 1989 . . . History will show that this day will be a symbol of shame, a day that the people will always remember. On this day, the government has ripped off the last shred of the veil covering its hideous visage. It has dispatched thousands of brutal troops and police, who have frenziedly attacked totally unarmed students and people, to suppress the students and people. We no longer hold out any hope whatsoever for this government. We now solemnly declare: if Li Peng's government is not brought down, China will perish and the people will no longer have any right to existence whatsoever.[24]

Eventually, the leaders of the CCP decided to take action. On the night of June 3–4, People's Liberation Army troops violently moved into central Beijing and Tiananmen Square, using tanks and armored personnel carriers to take the square and the surrounding streets back from the students. Unofficial estimates put the death toll as high as 3,000, although official estimates put the toll at about one-tenth of that number. Regardless of the actual death toll, the devastation wrought on the Party's reputation during the takeover was profound.

The Party leadership quickly turned its attention to strengthening ideological work after the military strike. Because of his open sympathy for the student demonstrators and hunger strikers, Zhao Ziyang was dismissed from his post, as Hu Yaobang had been two years earlier. Throughout the nation, ideological pluralism was denounced, and students were subjected to intense educational programs as well as year-long military training as a means for reestablishing ideological purity. One group of Beijing University students was even given a mandatory course on the military crackdown itself in order to convince them of the government's line. On the whole, however, these efforts seem to have been unconvincing, and few students remained committed to the Party line. Most disturbing to the Party leadership was the students' dramatic loss of faith in Marxism, which was in trouble well before the Tiananmen demonstrations.

The Tiananmen demonstrations and the subsequent crackdown have probably had the greatest effect on China's students, who are expected to eventually lead the nation in the future. The Party's version of the national myth, cultivated so carefully over the years, was destroyed by the Tiananmen events. The dissidents and many students have put forth their own version of the national myth and historical progression that envisions a post-Communist future. This version argues that China has not yet been released from the bondage of feudalism and tyranny. Yan Jiaqi, for example, argued that:

> In China Deng Xiaoping, Li Peng, and Yang Shangkun—those butchers of the people—shall not enjoy even a single day of peace and tranquility, for a massive transformation of China has been barely contained. In the not too distant future, those butchers will be brought to public trial, the one-party dictatorship will end in mainland China, a noncommunist government will be established there, and at long last the democratization of mainland China will open the way to China's reunification. I believe that in the twenty-first century a democratic and free federal republic will definitely be established in the great land of China.[25]

This vision of Yan's illustrates that it is not only the middle chapters of the national myth that are being rewritten, but also the concluding chapter. Many of the dissidents no longer see communism as China's destiny, and have pledged to bring about another destiny altogether.

Although the Party quickly restored some measure of social and political stability immediately after the Tiananmen demonstrations, the turmoil gave strength to the leftist elements within the government in their efforts to slow down the reforms, justifying this move as necessary to "maintain order and stability." To many in this group, the events of 1989 illustrated the errors of the overall reform agenda, and called for a strengthening of Party organs and discipline. A widespread campaign against a "peaceful evolution" toward capitalism sought to put a check on overzealous affection for the West. Zhao Ziyang remained under house arrest, as a message to the reformers that movements seeking to limit the Party's power would not be tolerated.

Deng Xiaoping, while he adamantly agreed that political reform was out of the question, argued for the acceleration of economic reforms. In the spring of 1992, he made a widely publicized trip to the boom towns of southern China's Guangdong province, where he officially declared that leftist errors were more dangerous than rightist errors. In addition, Deng promised that those who opposed the reform policies would leave the political stage. Deng's trip was designed to reaffirm the direction of the reforms, and reminded the leftists remaining in the government of their tenuous status.[26]

When the Fourteenth Party Congress opened in October, 1992, the Party was faced with serious rhetorical challenges. Not only did the reforms need ideological strengthening, but the legitimacy of the Party itself was open to question among significant portions of the population. The task of the Congress was to accelerate the reforms, while attempting to salvage whatever legitimacy the Party had remaining.

Over 2,000 delegates from throughout China attended the Fourteenth Party Congress. Jiang Zemin, Zhao Ziyang's replacement as Party chief, delivered the keynote address entitled "Accelerating Reform and Opening-Up."[27] Just as in previous congresses, the Fourteenth Congress attempted both to rewrite the national myth to portray the reforms as a fundamental part of the progression of history and establish an ideological orthodoxy based on the reform program. In addition, Jiang argued that historical progression dictated that the reforms were inevitable and part of the natural progression of history.

The Historical Necessity of Reform

Jiang began by outlining an historical account to demonstrate and affirm the historical significance of the Congress. Jiang argued that the present Congress had a vital task, that of accelerating the reforms:

The tasks of this Congress are, under the guidance of Comrade Deng Xiaoping's theory of building socialism with Chinese characteristics, to review the practical experience of the 14 years since the (Third Plenum) and to formulate a strategic plan for the next period. It is also the task of the congress to mobilize all Party comrades and the people of all nationalities to achieve still greater successes in building socialism with Chinese characteristics by further emancipating their minds and seizing this opportune moment to quicken the pace of reform, the opening to the outside world and the drive for modernization.[28]

He reminded the Congress of the version of the national myth cultivated over the years of the reforms, and again cited the Third Plenum of the Eleventh Central Committee in 1978 as a watershed in Chinese history:

Since the (Third Plenum), the Party and the people, guided by the theory of building socialism with Chinese characteristics, have been working hard to carry out reform. The whole nation has been reinvigorated, and historic changes have taken place across the land. The productive forces have been further emancipated, and the political situation of stability and unity has been steadily consolidated.[29]

Jiang noted the "revolutionary" impact of the 14 years of reform and declared the reform era to be a "new revolution," one based on economic modernization. Just as Mao and the first generation of revolutionaries had led China in a revolution to establish a democratic-socialist nation, Deng and the second generation led the Party and the people in "another great revolution, the goal of which is to further liberate and develop the productive forces."[30]

Foreign analysts had been using the phrase "second revolution" since at least the mid-1980s, but Chinese leaders were slow to use the phrase because it implied a drastic set of changes, something the reformers did not want to acknowledge. As I have argued in earlier chapters, the initial goal of the reformers was to legitimate the reforms as fully consistent with Mao's own directions, the policies of the early Party, and ideological orthodoxy. Jiang's proclamation of a second revolution signaled that an identifiable historical stage had begun at the 1978 Plenum, an era identified with Deng Xiaoping.

Just as historical progression established the inevitability of the first revolution, historical progression demanded the second: "The old economic structure has its historical origins and has played an important and positive role. With changing conditions, however, it has come to correspond less and less to the requirements of the modernization programme."[31] In addition, Jiang recounted the history of the reform program in an attempt to demonstrate how historical conditions prompted each new turn in the reform policies themselves.

Jiang reaffirmed the important role of Deng Xiaoping in promoting the reforms, and acknowledged Deng's role in formulating the ideological orthodoxy now known as "socialism with Chinese characteristics." There was little direct condemnation of Mao Zedong in Jiang's speech. Rather, Jiang recognized Mao as the core of the Party during the earlier revolution, and attributed the theoretical mistakes highlighted in the 1981 *Resolution* to forces other than Mao. Since the danger of a revived Maoism had largely passed, Jiang was able to appropriate the revolutionary legacy of Mao without endorsing any of Mao's policies. By arguing that Mao had brought about the first revolution, while Deng had birthed the second, Jiang was able to exclude Mao's legacy from any direct impact on present policy. The mythic legacy of Mao was preserved, while maintaining the historical distance necessary to preclude any unwelcome intrusion on policy, much as Sun Yat-sen had been cited as the founder of the a new era while separated from the Party he founded, the Kuomintang.

Although Jiang praised Deng as the founder of the second revolution, he emphasized that the reform program was the product of the Party. He argued that the legitimacy of the Party did not rest solely on its historical role in the 1930s and 1940s, but rather on its permanent role as the vanguard of history. No matter how many revolutions were needed, the Party would be the guide for the Chinese nation. By deemphasizing individuals and emphasizing the Party, Jiang's speech reinforced the legitimacy of the Party as the guiding force in society. "We must maintain long-term stability and make our country prosperous and strong. The key to all this is our Party, a party armed with Comrade Deng Xiaoping's theory of building socialism with Chinese characteristics."[32] Since the Party is armed with the correct ideology, the Party can be trusted to complete the revolution.

As already noted, however, the legitimacy of the Party was under fire because of the Tiananmen demonstrations. In response, Jiang provided an official explanation for the events of 1989. His portrayal of the "Tiananmen Incident," as it is referred to in official publications, is largely consistent with previous characterizations by Deng and others. It was important to continue to portray the Party as the direct agent of history, in line with the orthodox national myth. Jiang sought to maintain the mythic legitimacy of the Party by portraying the Party as one which, under the guidance of the people, sought to defend the people's interests against the enemies of socialism:

> In late spring and early summer of 1989, a political disturbance broke out, and the Party and the government, relying on the people, took a clear-cut stand against unrest. They quelled the counter-revolutionary violence in Beijing, defending the power of the socialist state and the fundamental interests of the people and ensuring the continued progress of reform, the opening up and modernization.[33]

This description of the events portrays the students and intellectuals not as courageous reformers attempting to bring about positive social change, but as counterrevolutionaries out to upset the very foundations of the Chinese state and the processes of modernization and reform. In fact, according to Jiang, these hooligans were out to disrupt the reforms, rather than encouraging them. It was not May Fourth heroes who took Tiananmen Square; it was a gang of traitors. In response, the people demanded action on the part of the Party and the government. The military suppression was not only heroic and correct, it was based on the true democratic impulses of the nation. By referring to the desires of the people that the demonstrations be crushed, Jiang sought to offset the "democratic" image that the students had attempted to portray. The demonstrators and hunger strikers could not have represented true democracy, because the people themselves demanded that the demonstrators be ousted from the square.

In addition to the challenge to the national myth from the Tiananmen events, the governing ideology, Marxism, was challenged as a result of the worldwide rejection of Marxism. Jiang was forced to explain not only the continued legitimacy of the Party, but also the legitimacy of Marxism as the governing ideology. If the entire Communist world was in the process of dismantling communism, then why was China still committed to its implementation? To answer this question, Jiang was forced to establish the priority of Marxism in matters of Chinese national development. He began by reaffirming the necessity of national independence in matters of socialist development:

> The Chinese Communist Party has always held that countries must maintain their independence in revolution and development and that the success of socialism in China depends essentially on ourselves, on the Chinese Party's theory and line, and on the united efforts of the Party and the people . . . In formulating this theory, the Party has for the first time given preliminary but systematic answers to a series of basic questions about how to build, consolidate, and develop socialism in a country with a backward economy and culture like China. It has also developed Marxism by introducing new ideas and viewpoints.[34]

The reversal of communism was not the concern of the Chinese, as it was clear that Marxism was the only path for China to take. Since Marxism had brought the democratic revolution to China, and Marxist theory had brought the economic reforms to China, there was no reason to consider any other ideological grounding. Jiang reaffirmed the inevitability of socialism, even in other countries:

> Socialism is a completely new system in the history of mankind. It is bound to replace capitalism—that is the general trend of social and historical development. Any new social system, as it is born, consolidated and developed, inevitably follows a zigzag course of struggles and sacrifices, of victories and defeats. Communists and the people in general will surely be tempered in this process and draw lessons from it, pushing socialism in the right direction.[35]

Jiang argued that socialism had suffered a temporary setback in Eastern Europe and the Soviet Union, but the ultimate progression of history would inevitably bring those nations back to socialism. In keeping with the Chinese national myth, Jiang had no alternative explanations. Historical progression cannot be set aside by the will of the people, just as the Mandate of Heaven was not contingent on human will. China's task was to continue to uphold and advance socialism until the realization of the ultimate socialist goal.

The Expansion of Ideological Orthodoxy

Besides reaffirming and expanding the mythic history of the Party, Jiang speech also expanded the parameters of ideological line to be followed in the process of modernization, that of the "socialist market economy." I argued in Chapter 4 that the doctrine of the primary stage of socialism was intended to account rhetorically for the introduction of capitalist economic elements into the Chinese economy. At the Fourteenth Party Congress, Jiang incorporated this theoretical innovation as well as Deng's earlier references to a "socialism with Chinese characteristics" to provide a fuller ideological grounding for the reform movement.

Although Deng's "socialism with Chinese characteristics" concept had been in currency for several years, it was a "theory" only in the loosest sense, a set of disparate concepts strung together. Essentially, Jiang's version draws together two distinct sets of ideas, those that had traditionally been a strong part of China's Marxist ideological foundations, as well as those theoretical innovations related to the reform agenda. For example, Jiang reaffirmed the traditional emphases on the primacy of socialism, of Marxism–Leninism–Mao Zedong Thought and the Four Cardinal Principles, the Communist Party, and the reunification of China, while reintroducing theoretical innovations, such as the theory of the primary stage of socialism. Thus, the theory enshrines into dogma the idea that socialism proceeds through stages, and that China is in the primary stage of socialism. This stage will last at least a hundred years, and the Party "must not divorce ourselves from it or try to skip this stage."[36]

In addition, Jiang reaffirmed that the very essence of socialism was to obtain modernization:

> In essence, the objective of socialism is to liberate and develop the productive forces, to eliminate exploitation and polarization, and ultimately to achieve common prosperity . . . In the final analysis, the criterion for judging the success of our work in various fields is whether it helps develop the productive forces of socialist society, strengthen the overall capacity of the country and improve the people's standard of living.[37]

This is a key ideological transformation. Socialism is now defined as the development of productive forces, rather than a system to guarantee egalitarianism. Whatever brings about development is thus socialism. Since modernization is the goal, restructuring must be the mechanism for change, and every opportunity for development should be seized, including those that lead to greater class differences:

> Poverty is not socialism, but it is impossible for everyone to become prosperous simultaneously. We must allow and encourage some areas and individuals to grow rich first, so that more and more areas and individuals will do so until common prosperity is eventually achieved.[38]

Jiang introduced another theoretical innovation when he argued that central planning was not a key characteristic of a socialist economic system:

> According to conventional thinking, a market economy is peculiar to capitalism, and a planned economy is the basic feature of socialism. Since the [third plenum], we have gradually freed ourselves from those conventional ideas and acquired a new understanding.[39]

Jiang identified "conventional thinking," or traditional Marxism, as flawed. There is nothing inherent in socialism that dictates central economic planning. If a market economy frees productive forces, then the market economy is socialistic, regardless of the impact on class structure.

Jiang credited Deng Xiaoping's talks during his tour of southern China earlier in the year with helping to break down the traditional understanding of the distinction between capitalism and socialism. Since planning exists under both socialist and capitalistic systems, and markets exist under both systems, then central planning should not be the defining characteristic of socialism. Jiang argued that this revelation was a stunning new notion: "This brilliant thesis has helped free us from the restrictive notion that the planned economy and the market economy belong to basically different systems."[40]

A more accurate distinction between socialism and capitalism, Jiang argued, would be the basis of ownership. In a socialist state, public ownership is predominant, with private ownership secondary. As long as the public sector is greater than the private sector, then a nation is socialistic. Although this is orthodox Marxism, Jiang introduces a key theoretical distinction. In his version, public ownership is not equivalent to public control. Rather, the processes of contract management, in which publicly owned enterprises are privately managed, will be the basis for administration.

In addition, publicly and collectively owned enterprises would not be spared market competition by the government. Instead, they would be forced into the market to compete with privately owned companies in order to maximize production and increase efficiency. The government would step out of the role of managing enterprises altogether, and take on a role of overall planning, regulation, inspection, and guidance. Thus, publicly owned industries would be subject to the forces that shape the private economy. Publicly owned enterprises would act as if they were privately owned.

The rhetorical significance of this new definition is that it allows market forces to be the primary instrument of control of economic decisions. The government would no longer guarantee that egalitarian values and traditional Marxist economic planning would be implemented, as the market was to be the prime consideration for economic decision-making. Beyond its role of regulation to make sure that there was no corruption, the government would no longer be involved with issues of production. With this understanding, economic forces and mechanisms that had previously been identified with capitalistic systems, such as stock markets, could now be grasped with equal vigor by socialist nations. Factories could compete for contracts, and were free to alter production if the market warranted. Individual economic strategies, even those that were clearly based on private ownership and capitalism, could be approved with zeal as long as the nation as a whole maintained the bulk of its enterprises as publicly owned.

The concept of a "socialist marketplace" is the economic parallel to the Chinese political doctrine of "one country, two systems," by which China promises to maintain the existing political structures of Hong Kong and Macau. The "one country, two systems" doctrine asserts that two separate systems of governance and economic relationships can peacefully coexist under socialism and Party rule. In the same way, the "socialist market" doctrine asserts that capitalism can thrive under socialism, to the enrichment of both systems. In addition, capitalistic enterprise is patriotic, in that it helps to guarantee the modernization of the nation. Entrepreneurs and capitalists, formerly imprisoned or persecuted as class enemies, were granted honor in a nation formally dedicated to the eventual elimination of capitalism. Jiang argued that by establishing and refining the socialist market economy, the superiority of socialism over capitalism would be conclusively demonstrated.[41]

Jiang was careful not to draw tight parameters around the concept, though. Rather, he allowed the theoretical laxity needed for further revision of ideological orthodoxy, as the need might arise. "As we test it in the course of practice, study new situations and solve new problems, we shall continue to enrich, refine and develop it."[42] Thus, a theory is established, but it is an open-ended theory, one that allows for as much refinement as possible. However, Jiang insisted on the legitimacy of the theory, as theory, and reaffirmed its necessity:

> [The theory] is the product of the integration of the fundamental tenets of Marxism–Leninism with the reality of present-day China and the special features of our times, a continuation and development of Mao Zedong Thought, a crystallization of the collective wisdom of the entire Party membership and the whole Chinese people, and an intellectual treasure belonging to them all.[43]

Jiang also addressed the problem of ideological errors that would disrupt China's movement toward socialism. He began by distinguishing between rightist errors and leftist errors. Rightist errors are "manifested chiefly in negating the Four Cardinal Principles, in pursuing bourgeois liberalization, and sometimes in creating political turmoil." Rightist errors were those traditionally identified as the enemy of the Party, which would seek to delay or deflect Marxism altogether.

Leftist errors, on the other hand, were "manifested chiefly in denying the correctness of the reform and the open policy, maintaining that the main danger of peaceful evolution toward capitalism comes from the economic sphere, and trying to distract us from the central task of economic development by emphasizing the need for class struggle."[44] Leftist errors, although they have always been present, compose a new set of enemies, since the attacks of the Party have always been directed toward rightist errors. Jiang explained that the chief danger facing the Party was Leftist errors, although rightist errors could also sidetrack the move to socialism.

Although Jiang warned cadres to look out for both types of errors, he identified leftist errors as the most dangerous to the Party and the process of reform. Such an attitude would have been unthinkable even a few years previously, so entrenched was Mao's attitude toward "rightists" and "capitalist-roaders." In short, what Jiang was saying was that more tolerance would be afforded the students who led the Tiananmen demonstrations than the remaining Maoists. Whereas the students would be controlled by political means, and the reforms kept on track, the devastation brought on by the leftists would be impossible to control, and could keep China in poverty forever.

This does not mean that Jiang in any sense proposed an opening of the political realm, or the free exchange of different perspectives. Although rightist errors would not be subject to the same scrutiny as leftist errors, the government and Party would actively police ideological orthodoxy. Jiang argued that only ideological education based on orthodox theory could guarantee national stability, thus reaffirming the role of the national myth and of ideology in cultivating socialist virtue:

> We should teach the people of all nationalities, especially young people, about the Party's basic line, about modern and contemporary history and about the present conditions of our country, fostering patriotism, community spirit and socialist ideology. Thus, they will come to prize national dignity, self-confidence and self-reliance. They will resist the corrosive influence of the decadent capitalist and feudal ideologies and cherish correct ideals, convictions and values.[45]

A strict emphasis on ideological education, then, would guarantee China's socialist future. It is interesting to note that Jiang's intrinsic connection of the national myth and ideological orthodoxy to the community values of patriotism, courage, and community spirit. Paralleling traditional Confucian thought, Jiang argued that virtue is dependent on ideology. As Jiang remarked at another point in his speech:

> the consolidation and development of socialism will require one generation after another of hard, persistent, unyielding struggle. The responsibilities are heavy and the road is long; our hopes must be placed on the young. We must win the youth if we are to win the future.[46]

Jiang's speech attempted to provide coherence to the disparate theoretical concepts guiding China's reforms. By introducing the "socialist market economy," Jiang freed China from the central planning that had precipitated the devastation and famine of the Great Leap Forward and other economic disasters. China's factories and businesses were free to pursue market forces wherever they might lead. Jiang's address legitimated a whole range of business enterprises, which were now only required to increase productivity.

Reaction to Jiang's speech was enthusiastic in the official Chinese press. An article in the *Beijing Review* argued that:

> It goes without saying that putting forward the new concept . . . represents a major theoretical breakthrough. It has broken down the outdated notion that a planned economy means socialism and a market economy capitalism.[47]

Deng, who had not been present for the bulk of Congress, showed up at the end to give his blessing on the events and told Jiang Zemin that the meeting had been a success.[48] Hong Kong analysts called the Congress a triumph for Deng Xiaoping in institutionalizing the reform program.[49]

This reaction was predictable. The real test of Jiang's speech, however, will be the speed with which new policies and enterprises develop, and the extent to which budding entrepreneurs trust that there will be no reversals, and that there really is room under a benevolent socialism for class distinctions to arise, for unequal economic development, and for the fuller enrichment of capitalism. Deng Xiaoping was rumored to be worried that Li Peng's 1993 National People's Congress report would endorse an economic cooldown, an event that did not occur.[50]

Conclusions

At the conclusion of the Fourteenth Party Congress, the reforms seemed to have broken out of the stagnation that had held them for quite some time. In March of 1993, Li Peng declared that modernization and economic growth were firmly on track, and noted that the 1980 gross domestic product would be quadrupled two years earlier than the year 2000, a goal of the government at least since the Thirteenth Party Congress. In addition, the Party seems to be poised to move into further reforms. Jiang attempted at the Fourteenth Party Congress to unify the disparate elements of "socialism with

Chinese characteristics," and this attempt has mainly served to eliminate central planning as a component of Marxism, thus removing only one barrier, albeit a major one, to the reforms. Jiang's phrase, "socialist market economy," was subsequently written into the Party Constitution in an attempt to solidify its orthodoxy, and to lessen the possibilities of a quick reversal of the policy.[51] The major theoretical strength of the rhetoric of legitimation is the change of focus toward economic empowerment and modernization, a theme shared by many non-Marxists. With this theme, it seems that China can remain formally committed to socialism without actually implementing traditional socialist economic mechanisms. Even though the nation will continue to proclaim its loyalty to socialism, market forces will guide economic decisions. Since socialism is now defined as the elimination of poverty, the only test of orthodoxy a policy is subjected to is that it spur greater economic growth.

Even these theoretical innovations do not eliminate all of the theoretical problems inherent in the reform process. For example, the Party is still upholding public ownership as the mainstay of China's economy, while publicly acknowledging that private ownership is normally more efficient. To capture the benefits of the private economy without denationalizing industries, the reform policies are designed to force the publicly owned industries to attempt to do business according to the rules of the private economy. This means, for example, that government-owned industries will no longer receive huge subsidies, but they will still be forced to meet some of the requirements of publicly owned enterprises, such as retaining unnecessary personnel. It remains to be seen if this type of arrangement is sustainable over a period of time.

Jiang's speech attempted to do more than spur economic growth, though; in addition, he attempted to reinvigorate the Party's ethos with the drama of the national myth. By arguing that the Party had turned a corner at the 1978 Third Plenum, Jiang attempted to portray the Party as the agent of modernization and continued economic progress. Since much of the nation no longer remembered the early virtues of the Party, Jiang was forced to attempt to update the image of the Party as a liberator, although it was no longer clear to the younger generation exactly who or what was oppressing the nation.

The difficulty in Jiang's task was that few people remained who could personally testify to the corruption and oppressive nature of the Kuomintang. Based on survey research on student attitudes in China, for example, Stanley Rosen argues that:

In their appeals to the glories of the pre-1949 Communist Revolution and their revival of the campaigns to study the selfless revolutionary heros of pre–Cultural Revolution China, they have conceptualized a society that no longer exists, raising issues far removed from the concerns of Chinese students in the 1990s.[52]

The government has stepped up its ideological education programs in order to capture the newest generation of middle school students, with the hopes of making the national myth compelling again. This will be a difficult task, though, since the current generation remembers the chaos of the Cultural Revolution and the campaigns against Western influence far more vividly than they remember Western imperialism and the oppressive economic structures of the past. Liberation from political and economic oppression brought by the Party was to a large extent no longer relevant to younger Chinese.[53]

Even if the younger generation is willing to suspend their disbelief of the greater political freedom that has come with socialism, the government has to convince the young that the Communist Party has led China into greater economic opportunity, a task made more difficult by the increased exposure to the outside world, including Taiwan. When the citizens of the mainland contemplate their relative economic advancement compared to the Chinese living on Taiwan, the abilities of the CCP to lead the nation to prosperity are not so self-evident. Anecdotal evidence abounds of Chinese who were told as they were growing up about the poor people in America and Taiwan, only to find out through increased exposure that the real poverty was in China. In large part then, students and intellectuals in particular view the Party as a "gang of the old," to use Liu Binyan's phrase. The gang of the old, in this view, has done little but to stifle the creativity and the aspirations of China's population.

The task facing Jiang and the other leaders of China is to recreate the mythic legitimacy of liberators. The rhetoric of the reforms has illustrated the ways in which the Party has attempted to redefine liberation. By defining the second revolution as economic revolution, the Party makes some headway with the citizens who are eager for newly obtainable wealth. It remains to be seen, however, if economic liberation is as powerful a mythic element as political and personal liberation was in Mao's version of the national myth.

Perhaps most important, Jiang's speech failed to account adequately for the ghosts of Tiananmen Square. This event will be a defining moment for future generations, although it is difficult to predict which version, either the government's or the demonstrators', will finally be accepted into the national myth. By portraying the demonstrators as "enemies of reform," Jiang maintained coherence within the version of Party history preferred by the Party, but reaffirmed the convictions of many Chinese that the leaders of the Party were out of touch with reality. Since many Chinese journalists were in sympathy with the students, there was a significant period of reporting that favored the students' position. Liu Binyan writes that more than half a million intellectuals from various cultural organizations and media outlets participated in the demonstration.[54]

The Party's version was presented most fully after the crackdown, and became particularly compelling in areas where there was little access to foreign media coverage. By that time, however, the damage to the reputation of the Party had been done. The Central Committee confirmed that the verdict on Zhao Ziyang's responsibility for the demonstrations was just, just days before the Fourteenth Congress opened. The confirmation of Zhao's sentence brought disappointment to those who had hoped for a reversal, and illustrated the incommensurability of the two versions of the events.[55]

Part of Jiang's rhetorical strategy to maintain the Party's early heroic legitimacy in the face of the Tiananmen disaster was to emphasize the economic accomplishments of the Party. Thus, he chose to downplay individual persons and focus on the accomplishments of the Party as a whole. For example, by arguing that it was the Party, rather than Deng Xiaoping, that had instituted the reforms, that had opened up the nation, and that had brought economic prosperity, the Party maintained its claims that the Party had truly brought liberation.

Both before and since the 1992 Party Congress, the Party has also attempted to maintain the mythic legitimacy of the Party by creating a heroic image of Deng Xiaoping. Regardless of earlier public campaigns to break China's patterns of emperor worship, something of a personality cult has developed around Deng. As political turmoils have subsided, more and more references have been made to "Eminent Personage Deng," *Deng Da Ren*. A biography of Deng published in the official *Beijing Review* to coincide with the Party Congress was entitled "The Man Who Makes History." The article introduced Deng by stating:

At age 88, legendary Deng leads a far-reaching and inspiring revolution, which ushers in the stablest and most prosperous era in the contemporary history of China, and impresses the whole world with its impetus, irreversibility and promise."[56]

The article further refers to Deng as "the helmsman of the country" and "the father of reform." Deng himself was reported to have resisted establishing a formal declaration of "Deng Xiaoping Thought" in an effort to minimize the ramifications of identifying economic progress as the result of one man's efforts.[57] Deng Rong's recent biography of her father, entitled *My Father Deng Xiaoping*, attempts much the same: to relegitimate the Party by reawakening the national myth within China's youth.[58]

At the conclusion of the Fourteenth Party Congress, then, the reforms seemed firmly entrenched ideologically and organizationally. Few envision any realistic scenarios in which the reforms could be reversed. Jiang's pronouncement of a socialist market economy seems to merely be an official recognition of the inevitable. The national myth, however, remains tentative and fragile. The "Tiananmen Incident," as it is referred to in official Party discourse, remains an open wound in the mythic legacy of the Party. In the final chapter, I will turn to an examination of the trajectory of the rhetoric legitimizing the reforms and make some comments regarding what can be learned about the rhetoric of legitimation from the example of China's economic reforms.

6 Chinese Political Discourse and the Rhetoric of Legitimacy

> *If names are not rectified, then language will not be in accord with truth. If language is not in accord with truth, then things cannot be accomplished. If things cannot be accomplished, then ceremonies and music will not flourish. If ceremonies and music do not flourish, then punishment will not be just. If punishments are not just, then the people will not know how to move hand or foot. Therefore the superior man will give only names that can be described in speech and say only what can be carried out in practice. With regard to his speech, the superior man does not take it lightly. That is all.*
>
> "The Analects of Confucius," 13.3[1]

So far, we have attempted to demonstrate that the rhetorical campaign to legitimate the Chinese economic reforms has been based in large part on a creative retelling of the national history and the gradual alteration of ideological orthodoxy. The difficulties faced in actual implementation of the reforms have been offset in large part by the rhetorical use of correct "names" for the reforms, and hence the establishment of a historical and ideological space for them. In spite of a lack of attention paid to Asian rhetorical practices from Western scholars in the past, it is clear from this example that Asian politics, no less than Western, places an absolute primacy on language and rhetoric. Robert Oliver has argued that in the West, rhetoric has been considered so important that it merited separate discussions (hence Aristotle separating rhetoric from politics, ethics, etc.). Among Eastern cultures, however, "rhetoric has been considered so important that it could not be separated from the remainder of human knowledge."[2] The manner in which an idea is expressed is inseparable from the idea itself. In this chapter, we will attempt to clearly sum up what we have identified as the elements of Chinese political discourse and the role of that discourse in Chinese society, as well as look at the implications of the nature of Chinese political discourse in China for the nation's future.

The fifth century B.C. philosopher Confucius was once asked what his first priority as a newly appointed government official would be. His answer, quoted at the start of the chapter, was that his first priority would be the rectification, or correction, of names. Confucius contended that when names accurately described the concept, and concepts conformed to their proper names, society would function properly. When kings behaved as kings and subjects behaved as subjects, harmony would reign. Inherent in Confucius' understanding is the contention that linguistic issues have an ethical component, that proper names lead to correct action. Language is as much moral as it is analytical. The first and primary goal of the government, then, was to accurately describe the world. Once the proper names were given, society would function properly.

Language, then, serves as an Archimedian lever, a stable point from which the entire world can be moved. Whoever controls the naming process, the "word," controls the world. Language, and linguistic description, is primary to all questions of politics, economics, and human motivation. Rhetorical action is at the core of all other human activity, echoing Kenneth Burke's contention that symbolic activity is the core of all human motivation.

China's current leaders are firmly convinced that anything can be done, within the limits of the material world (which puts them at odds with Mao, who did not seem to regard the material world as an impediment to true reality), as long as it has the right linguistic foundation. The goal has been to name the reform agenda in such a way as the reforms would be accelerated. The naming process itself is crucial to the success of the reforms.

In many ways, the rhetoric of the reforms parallel the reform process itself. The ad hoc implementation of the reforms are similar to the ad hoc attempts at justifying them. In the case of the Chinese reforms, the implementation of policy has preceded the development of theory, rather than theory guiding policies. The language to express the theory has been inconsistent and is always attempting to catch up with the policies themselves. From a rhetorical perspective, the periodic policies of retrenchment and shoring up are not so much derived from economic necessity, but because the proper rhetorical foundation had not yet been found to support the actual reform policies. Research institutes have been set up for the express purpose of exploring the theoretical basis for the reforms, in short, to find the proper names to express the policies. Such a diligence over rhetorical precision is in striking contrast to the attempts of Western politicians to study the rhetorical impact of phrases, not for their precision, but for their responsiveness within the population.

When we take a longitudinal glance at the Chinese reform process, we see a clear trajectory of the justifications themselves. In much the same way as time lapse photography reveals the dramatic changes in scenery, this analysis of the rhetorical trajectory of legitimation reveals the dramatic changes in that rhetoric. The early justificatory rhetoric relied primarily on the first principles of Mao's authority and the national myth. The justification then advanced to an argument from historical progression and finally to an altogether different reconceptualization and definition of socialism. The common threads running through each of these stages are the continuous revising and retelling of history and a continuous subtle revision of ideological orthodoxy. Each new retelling of the national myth focuses on liberation and features a slightly different shading to the characters. Over time, these slight changes have a dramatic effect, as the hues and tones slowly change to completely alter the picture. The pure and noble, like the mythic Mao, become sullied, while the impure and ignoble, like Deng Xiaoping, become pure. The process of using subtle gradations of gray allows the Party to eventually alter the places of both black and white. The central feature of the myth, revolution and liberation, however, remains stable.

The ideological grounding of the government has similarly been subtly altered. Mao Zedong Thought is still enshrined in the Constitution as the guiding theory of the revolution, but the substance of Mao Zedong Thought has changed. Much of Mao's policies are discarded while the teachings of Mao's rivals are inserted into the body of Mao Zedong Thought. Ideological orthodoxy, as any other orthodoxy, is an elusive concept, as "orthodox" only makes sense within any given historical framework. Outside of that framework, what was once orthodox may be merely anachronistic. We see a vast difference between the *legitimating* power of ideology and the actual content of that ideology.

Perhaps the most important contribution this type of analysis can make is that it causes us to briefly turn our attention away from organizational and political factors and to focus on the rhetorical elements of governmental legitimation. Although they are often criticized for being "out of touch" with the heart of China's people, it is clear that current Party leaders are well aware of the importance of rhetorically institutionalizing the reforms. Deng Xiaoping, as the architect for the radical ideological about-face after Mao's death, is well aware of the potential for reversal of his own ideological legacy and his policies. He has attempted to minimize this potential by portraying the reforms as the inevitable progression of history and the fulfillment of ideological orthodoxy; in short, by grounding the reforms in something other than the personal legitimacy of Deng Xiaoping.

We have argued so far that both the national myth and ideological orthodoxy are necessary for legitimation, and that both require constant revision in order to stay relevant in changing social and historical settings. At this point in the reform process, the continued legitimacy of the Party rests on the national myth, while the prestige of ideological orthodoxy guarantees the legitimacy of the reforms. Ideologically, the reforms seem to be entrenched. The Party is firmly committed to "socialism with Chinese characteristics" and the establishment of a "socialist market economy." The power of these formulations lies largely in their ambiguity. No one can envision what it would mean to oppose "socialism with Chinese characteristics," and thus the formulation itself seems largely empty, though not without rhetorical force. "Socialist market economy," likewise, can mean pretty much whatever the national leadership wants it to mean. Finally, the practice criterion, that "practice is the sole criterion of truth," has been established as the dominant ideological theme for the period of the reforms, lending strength to pragmatic politics and economics.

In spite of its certainty, however, the "practice" criterion holds little promise for Chinese dissidents and Western advocates of human rights because in the current scheme, "practice" refers to pragmatic economic policies. In spite of its economic progress, China has a dismal record as it relates to the political and religious freedom of its citizens. In fact, if the reformers are correct in asserting that prosperity will bring greater social stability, then Marx was wrong, in that it is actually the case that "prosperity is the opiate of the masses."

In spite of these weaknesses, it seems that the ideological legitimacy of the reforms is settled. The power of Deng's new version of history is in large part based on a desire of the populace to stabilize society and move beyond the upheavals of the Cultural Revolution. It is difficult to imagine new generations demonstrating for a return to the good times of the Cultural Revolution and poverty. Instead, by institutionalizing prosperity and wealth as the legitimate utopia to which Chinese may aspire, Deng has solidified his reforms more powerfully than legions of soldiers could. But here we are confronted with a paradox: The deepening of the reforms constantly puts the legitimacy of the Party at risk as the contrast between the history of the Party and the reform policies grows wider. Even the most radical critics of the government do not object to prosperity; their objection is to the role of the Party in governing China and the ability of the Party to bring about true prosperity.

With the rise of new generations, the national myth put forth by the Party no longer seems quite as compelling, in large part because the oppression before the 1949 Revolution has passed from the collective memory to a greater degree than have memories of the tyranny of the Cultural Revolution. Insofar as the contributions of the Party to the nation are forgotten, it can be expected that the restlessness brought on by dynamic economic change will erode the political foundations of the currently constituted Party. Hence Deng Rong's biography of her father Deng Xiaoping devotes almost 500 pages in the English version to the heroic efforts of the Party to achieve liberation, with nary a word about ideology.[3] Deng Rong's book is a clear attempt to preserve the legitimacy of the Party for a new generation by reviving the myth of liberation.

In the event that attempts such as Deng Rong's fail, the only way that the CCP can maintain its legitimacy is to reconstitute itself rhetorically as the epic hero of a different revolution, the economic revolution. This myth-making process has begun, as we mentioned in the previous chapter. Deng has been identified as the "architect" of the new revolution, one as far-reaching as the world has ever seen. An article on Deng in the official *Beijing Review* stated that "legendary Deng leads a far-reaching and inspiring revolution . . . and impresses the whole world with its impetus, irreversibility and promise."[4] A myth built on economic progress is much more difficult to sustain, though, than one built on the history of the Chinese revolution, based on national dignity and a release from oppression.

It could very well be that the processes of economic and technological modernization will destroy the vitality of the national myth. Robert Bellah argues that modernization virtually destroyed Japan's national myth and replaced it with a corporate ideology whose sole purpose was to continue economic growth and prosperity.[5] It is entirely possible that the roots of the national myth would be destroyed by the economic and material benefits of modernization themselves, such as thousands of fax machines all over the nation undercutting official propaganda during the Tiananmen Square demonstrations. Were this to occur, we have not yet seen what new national myth would arise to replace it.

A more likely problem facing the Chinese leadership is that one important element of the national myth, the doctrine of historical progression, will eventually undermine the legitimacy of the Party. Just as the ancient doctrine of the Mandate of Heaven justified the overturning of recent dynasties, so the doctrine of historical progression could ultimately be used to argue that the Chinese Communist Party had its role in history, but has now outlived its historical purpose. A revised national myth might argue that the Communist Party played an important historical role, that of releasing China from old cultural and economic patterns, but that a new hero has arrived to lead China to the next stage of history. To those planning for a global Chinese economy of the twenty-first century, the Party seems to be something of a curious anachronism, a dinosaur from a previous age still attempting to enforce its rule. This attitude is current among many Chinese intellectuals grateful for the national dignity restored by the Communists, but chafing under the rigid political control of the Party. A key plank of the national myth, that of historical progression, could be the internal time bomb that will destroy the legitimacy of the Party for ever.

The Language of History

One significant conclusion that arises from the Chinese example is that legitimation is grounded in historical positioning. This means more than has often been understood by referring to "traditional" authority, however. Modernizing, fully secular states rely on history to establish the character and the legitimation of the state. With the rise of new generations in China, we might reasonably believe that historical narratives would lose importance, in favor of rational, or even technological, grounds of legitimation. The modernizing process in China has fooled many Western observers into believing that historical positioning is irrelevant in today's "technocratic" China. Deng Xiaoping's authority for several years was viewed in precisely that light, as an authority based on modern, technocratic bases. The actual fact, though, is that in China, historical narrative remains a primary component of political discourse. The telling and revision of history remains a highly political act, as each new revision of the national myth indicates the political stand of the teller. Although details of this myth are frequently in revision, the broad parameters are unchanging. Ideological or political innovations must conform to the broad parameters of the myth in order to even seem credible.

Moreover, historical positioning is of paramount importance in establishing the moral authority of rulers. For this reason, it seems that every significant player that comes to the political scene must find a historical parallel to account for his or her existence. The Beijing students and intellectuals of 1989, for example, continually compared themselves to the May Fourth Movement of 1919. Political leaders go to great lengths to either appropriate historical analogies or argue why other analogies do not apply to them. It is for this reason that minor historical arguments assume tremendous significance, as illustrated by Mao's attack on the historian Wu Han in the 1960s. Wu had written essays and plays about the Ming Dynasty official Hai Rui, who had courageously remonstrated the Emperor and subsequently was dismissed from his post. Mao, as well as most of the Chinese leadership, correctly assessed the articles as trying to build sympathy for Peng Dehuai, the army marshal whom Mao had dismissed for his open criticism of the Great Leap Forward.[6] The arguments themselves are not as important as the political statement that is being made through them.

If there is no historical analogy for an event of a party, it is difficult to explain its existence. Unless the national myth includes an open chapter, it is next to impossible to insert one. Perhaps one reason that the Chinese leadership (and many of the dissidents, in spite of their promises) cannot conceive of a multiparty democracy, and the reason that this type of government has taken so long to gain a footing in Taiwan, is that the very idea of such a system is incompatible with the political myth of the revolution and historical progression. The myth does not allow for competing parties to cooperatively lead the nation out of oppression and poverty; it only allows for one heroic Party, usually reduced to one heroic person, either Sun Yat-sen, Chiang Kai-shek, or Mao Zedong. Even to entertain talk of competing parties is to deny the revolutionary history of the nation and shatter the basis of legitimation. To many of China's leaders, then, one might as well call for total anarchy as call for open elections. It is not only the Communist Party that is being challenged, but the very basis of government. Only in recent years has it even been legal in Taiwan to seriously consider the possibility that Taiwan and the People's Republic could be two different nations. The People's Republic still views this talk as treachery, because the open admission of two different nations would seriously undermine the myth of the revolution.

A historical example helps to illustrate this further. Historians have an easy task in criticizing Chiang Kai-shek's relationship with the Communist Party during the Civil War. Chiang is criticized for fighting the Communist armies while the Japanese controlled large portions of China as well as for refusing to allow the CCP any legitimacy as an opposition political party. What is not taken into account in these criticisms is that in the worldview inherited from China's Confucian past, the national myth allowed for no such entity as a loyal opposition. Since ideological variance implies disloyalty, even treachery, Chiang's energies were directed at eliminating the "traitor within" before focusing on the outside enemy, much as one would attempt to conquer cancer before one tried to vanquish outside foes. It is significant that Chiang's "reconciliations" with the Communist Party were always driven by absolute necessity, such as the need for U.S. military aid, which was conditional on Chiang's cooperation with the CCP.

Persuasive political rhetoric, then, is that which makes the most of the available roles in the national myth and makes the revision of history more compelling. It is not so much that Mao and Deng set out to become the "new emperors" in Salisbury's phrase, but that the entire political culture imposed those roles on those occupying the leading position in the government.[7] We see a similar concern for historical validity even within Western governments. Leaders of both left and right appeal to historical events or personalities as evidence of the legitimacy of policies and political actors. This evidence demonstrates that the national myth remains a compelling part of the legitimation process of any nation.

In order to critique claims to legitimacy, then, we must identify a means for critiquing historical narratives. Walter Fisher's twin criterions of "narrative coherence" and "narrative fidelity" serve as a sound starting point from which to more carefully examine the persuasive power of the national myth.[8] According to Fisher, the rhetorical power of any narrative is based on the degree to which the narrative has internal coherence and fidelity to the experiences of hearers. Applying these criteria to the Chinese national myth, it is clear that the myth is compelling for those Chinese who lived through the period of foreign domination, but lacking in fidelity for younger generations, who have only known the strong arm of the CCP. The national myth further suffers from a lack of coherence, caused by the ever-changing external necessities to revise the myth and orthodoxy to allow for innovation in the economic sphere. The degree to which this lack of coherence can be overcome is the degree to which the rhetoric of legitimation will be successful.

The Language of Ideology

Besides historical positioning within the national myth, we have also argued for the legitimating power of ideology. Ideological content is continually in flux, but the legitimating force of ideology remains fairly stable. We will turn briefly to examining how language and linguistic formulations form ideology, particularly in China. One key way of managing the "fluctuations of orthodoxy," or stabilizing the content of ideology, is to limit the linguistic formulations. If words and word orders are limited, there is little room for variance or change in meaning. Ideological innovation is limited by the very fact that subtle changes in word usage and word order, and hence, meanings, are not allowed. Since there is no outlet for heterodox word usage or meanings, governors feel content that no serious ideological challenge to authority can arise.

Moreover, theories are themselves implied by linguistic formulations. Since certain formulations can be decreed illegal, so can the theories themselves. In using a formulation incorrectly or creatively, a party sets itself up for charges of sedition. For example, after Mao's death, Deng and others (notably, those who had been labeled as capitalist-roaders) saw to it that the notion of a "capitalist-roader" was theoretically repudiated, thereby establishing that the term itself had no meaning. Since the term had no meaning, it was meaningless to use it. Anyone who used the term, then, was arguing that Mao's ideology of the late 1960s and early 1970s was "correct," and would risk punishment by the government.

The practical consequences of this are enormous, and explain the importance of the government putting out periodic lists of "correct" formulations for use in the media. Potential rivals to government authority must somehow include themselves in the political stage without undermining the dominant ideology. It is difficult to be seen as somehow "different" from other political figures when a common political language is used. One way to get around this conformity is to use different "code words" or phrases that favor a certain emphasis, without implying a negation of orthodoxy. This is why it often seems that rhetoric serves merely to mask factional loyalties, as Lucian Pye has argued.[9] However, it is not factional loyalties that are hidden by the rhetoric, but ideologies.

Those in the West also recognize the role of language in implying ideology; for example, "law and order" conservatives or "compassionate" liberals. Politicians attribute deficiencies in an opponent's moral character, and thereby deny political legitimacy, based on the words they use in political discourse. Political actors find linguistic formulations that seem to codify far-ranging ideas, sympathies, and values, and are quick to point out that certain politicians either do or do not embody what the word means, seemingly hoping to revive Confucius' campaign to rectify names. One key difference between the West and China, however, is that in the West, politicians use language to satisfy key constituencies and likely voters and thereby gain votes, with little responsibility to higher leaders. In China, to refuse to use or to misuse the officially approved language is to set oneself against the preferred ideology and mark oneself as a traitor. Hence, Li Peng's ability to hang on to his job hinges in large part on his willingness to use the language of Deng Xiaoping.[10]

The Role of Audience in Chinese Politics

Perhaps the key difference between Chinese and Western political discourse relates to the role of that discourse in terms of the overall political process, particularly, the role of the discourse in influencing an audience. In what way does the discourse of the regime, represented by speeches and documents emanating from Beijing, actually *influence* people? What evidence is there that the citizenry actually *believe* the discourse? It seems from the examples so far that political rhetoric in China seeks to provide rationales for policy, rather than induce belief. The definition of public ideology does not necessitate public adherence to that ideology. The speeches that arise from Party congresses and other important meetings are important not so much to persuade the nation as to delineate the new political line and reveal the compromise/consensus of top Party offi-

cials and provide clues into acceptable belief and behavior, and ultimately, to *create* a political reality.

In order to fully understand the role of political rhetoric, we
must first clearly distinguish between particular audiences of such
political discourse. We will mention three primary audiences, each of
which responds in a markedly different way to official political discourse; government personnel, including the highest leaders; intellectuals; and workers and peasants.

For those involved in high-level politics, it is clear that political
discourse is often only a language game, and the rhetoric that accom-
panies movements is taken very lightly. As noted China scholar
Lucian Pye argues, rhetorical proclamations serve largely to signal
factional infighting.[11] Political leaders use slogans and campaigns to
demonstrate alignments and trends in the government. A skilled
political observer can determine political trends from reading news-
paper headlines as conclusively as one used to be able to determine
changes in the line of the Soviet Union by studying May Day Parade
photographs. The frequency with which certain pronouncements
appear in the news is an accurate indicator of the relative stability of
the central government. The government uses slogans and phrases to
send out powerful warnings against dissent, veiled in vague and
ambiguous definitions.

To say that political rhetoric is used for political advantage
does not mean that leaders do not actually believe their discourse,
but rather, that belief is secondary to social impact. Chinese Communist leaders do believe that language changes social conditions,
and if saying something achieves an impact, then it is correct. A
statement is scientific if it achieves the desired impact, not if it can
be objectively proven. As Alan Liu argues, "The underlying assump-
tion of the Communist Party is that the social effect of news or
information is much more important than the truthfulness."[12] To
argue about whether or not a political leader believes his or her own
speech is to introduce a metaphysical component to a purely social
and political process, a component that is neither necessary nor
helpful. In a Western context, the question might have meaning;
this is not necessarily so in China. A more appropriate question is
what impact the speech has on the nation.

In the Chinese political context, words can become increasingly convoluted and paradoxical. China, officially a "people's
democracy," embraces a "dictatorship of the proletariat." The government equally stresses both "openness to the outside world" and

opposition to "bourgeois liberalization" and "spiritual pollution." Western analysts often find themselves misunderstanding both the meaning and the position of Chinese leaders when they assume that one clearly believes that which he has said.

For intellectuals, particularly those outside of the power structures, political discourse has a slightly different function. Perry Link argues that for this group, political language is primarily a means of gaining access to power.[13] Regardless of how true the statements are, they are necessary—as a sort of code—for gaining entry into the larger conversation in the nation. When one uses a language far removed from that official code established in Beijing, one is increasingly isolated from access to influence. Language is not a tool of expression, but an instrument of aggression and defense. Intellectuals will use the same formulations as the government, not in any attempt to deceive, but because in order to be heard one must use these formulations.

One way to illustrate this argument is to provide a negative example. The Tiananmen demonstrations demonstrated what happens when political actors in China reject the preferred idiom. Students and intellectuals involved in the 1989 demonstrations rejected the official discourse, and in doing so established themselves as enemies of the state. They insisted on a real "democracy" and argued that the Communist Party was villainous, rather than heroic. In rejecting the "people's democracy," students were being "antirevolutionary." When the *Renmin Ribao* editorial on April 26, 1989 referred to the demonstrations as "turmoil," the students were horrified and demanded a revision. As Deng Xiaoping later said, "What some people opposed was this word; what they demanded revised was this word."[14] The effect of this polarizing language was that the demonstrations quickly escalated into an all-out war between the government and the students, finally settled on the night of June 3–4. Deng Xiaoping is said to have remarked that if the students were not quickly defeated, the entire CCP leadership would be beheaded, reflecting his very real fears of the student's intentions.

If political language is utilitarian for both intellectuals and government leaders, then it is transformative for the larger masses of Chinese citizens. Language, for this group, has one primary function, that of justification. It transforms black into white and white into black. It both legitimates and delegitimates. For this audience, who for centuries have been subject to the whims of their leaders, political discourse serves as a map in that it can guide one to correct behavior and provide a means of understanding. That which has been designated as "socialist" is now legal and ethical, and those who understand are safe from governmental intrusion. Titles matter, not because they are true, but because they open doors. The vast social and economic changes that come over China within an inexplicably short time can be explained as a function of the power of the word. For example, the overnight transition to the communes in 1957–1958 were due largely to Mao's endorsement, and the explosion of small scale private enterprise in the 1980s have been due to the new political discourse that legitimates them. Chairman Mao's off-hand remark that "It is right to rebel" opened the floodgates for the vast cultural upheaval of the Cultural Revolution.

To express this in a different way, Chinese political rhetoric is not apologetic, in the sense of seeking to induce belief; nor is it dogmatic—it is not an attempt to actually explore the tenets of the faith. Rather, it is hortatory, justificatory, and educational in that it exhorts, justifies, and teaches the public about proper political stances. It is also utilitarian in that it is used defensively; it is meant to protect a speaker from accusations of heresy and treachery. By providing a compelling ideological grounding for policies, officials are protected from the chaos that periodically sweeps through China, carrying off all who are not firmly rooted in orthodoxy.

It is this that is the key difference between Western and Chinese political discourse. Western political discourse presupposes to some degree the idea of persuasion, rooted in rationality. The tradition of rhetorical analysis presumes that political rhetoric is an argument at its core, designed to impress an audience. Chinese political actors would not deny that persuasion does take place; in fact, they count on the persuasive power of rhetoric to move the nation. However, Chinese political rhetoric seems to presuppose a much more utilitarian purpose, that of justifying. Persuasion arises from justification. A rhetorical analysis of Chinese political discourse must begin with a recognition that the argument is secondary to the impact. Political commitments and action are presumed, rather than derived from rhetorical action. It is not so much the case that rhetoric persuades disinterested observers, but rather it exhorts people with inherent political positions and convictions. Rhetoric reconciles, it justifies, it explains. And in doing so, it allows us to change the world.

This raises one other important conclusion regarding political discourse in China, that of effectiveness. Rhetorical effectiveness has traditionally been understood as that which persuades. If, as I have argued, political discourse is not primarily designed to persuade, but to justify, then we must reconceptualize rhetorical effectiveness. I would propose a broader standard for effectiveness, that rhetoric is effective when it clearly resolves the conflicts and contradictions inherent in political situations. We must revise Aristotle's definition of rhetoric as the faculty of observing the available means of persuasion to the faculty of observing the available means of explaining. We can refer back to Fisher's narrative paradigm for help in formulating this: Political discourse is effective when it enables a government or any other political agency to logically resolve conflicts in mythic and ideological coherence and fidelity. As we rethink our conception of rhetorical effectiveness in political discourse, perhaps we will be attuned to some of the more subtle elements in our own political rhetoric, which we have previously overlooked in our focus on persuasion.

Political Legitimacy and Post-Tiananmen Social Change

We now come to an obvious question regarding the impact of China's political discourse on the future of a nation undergoing drastic change. Will the decline of the national myth and the corruption of ideological orthodoxy mean that China will finally enter into a democratic, market-oriented age? And what of international attempts to force some concessions on China in social and political realms? Are these doomed to failure, or can foreign nations still hope to influence China? Some Western analysts have prematurely concluded that the revolutionary bases of legitimacy are no longer relevant to society, given the decidedly technocratic nature of the top leadership and their commitment to reform. The Beijing correspondent for the *Los Angeles Times*, for instance, wrote that "China's successor-generation leaders face the cold knowledge that ideology and revolutionary prestige, two old pillars of the regime, are dead. Only economic progress can sustain their legitimacy."[15]

If our earlier contentions were correct, however, that the rhetoric shapes the politics rather than vice versa, we must rethink this conclusion. If the national myth and ideological formulations play such an important part in creating political consciousness, then that will necessarily affect the type of political changes that can occur. We have previously stated that the early mythic legacy of the revolution is largely forgotten, as is a societal ideological consensus; but it is important to remember that the Party has attempted to rebuild each of these components of legitimacy. The current "third generation" of top leaders, such as Jiang Zemin, were not direct participants in the Long March but they still have an enormous investment in the tremendous rhetorical appeal of the national myth, and seek to continually update both myth and orthodoxy to guarantee their legitimacy.

Indeed, the one group that would seem most likely to want to destroy the traditional bases of legitimacy—dissidents—now largely based outside of China, rely as heavily on the "two pillars" (national myth and ideology) of legitimacy as firmly as the Beijing leadership. To illustrate this, we will turn to one of the better-known dissidents, Yan Jiaqi. Yan clearly assumes the continuance both of the national myth and ideological certainty in his intellectual autobiography, *Towards a Democratic China*.

Yan accepts the dominant myth of progressive revolution and liberation, but insists that the stages of human history are ideological stages, rather than economic ones. His famous essay "Religion, Reason, and Practice: Visits to Three Courts of Law," published in the *People's Daily* in 1978, played an influential role in establishing the definition of practice as the sole criterion of truth, and giving impetus to Deng's reform faction.[16] Yan argued that there have been three important criterions of truth throughout history. The first, exemplified in sixteenth-century Italy, was that truth is found in religion. Yan finds that this perspective stifled creativity and knowledge and was oppressive. The second, exemplified by Enlightenment France, was that truth is to be found in reason. The final and conclusive criterion is that practice is the sole criterion of truth, as exemplified through an imaginary journey to twenty-first century Beijing, where prosperity and technological progress are abundant.

In Yan's understanding, then, the national myth still serves as an unfolding morality play, the purpose of which is liberation from dark thinking. The goal of revolution is to liberate people from oppression, albeit oppression of an intellectual nature. Historical progression dictates that there should be a a natural evolution in the basis of authority from religion, which is unreliable and oppressive, to reason, which is more humane but still unverifiable, to practice, which is both humane and verifiable. The "practice" criterion for truth, or science, will ultimately be the final ideology.

Yan asserts four convictions regarding the absoluteness of science: (1) that science is based on practice, (2) that every phenomena can be understood through science, (3) that scientific ideas are clear and truth is plain and straightforward, and (4) that there is no problem that science itself cannot solve.[17] These arguments reveal a fundamental belief that science is the absolute basis of authority, as absolute as Marxism–Leninism–Mao Zedong Thought was to earlier thinkers. One would expect that Yan, one of China's foremost political scientists and a philosopher, would be somewhat more reflective about the inherent ambiguity of science, but a self-critical philosophy of science appears nowhere in his work. Political legitimacy, to Yan Jiaqi and other dissidents, is a legitimacy based on science, with a universal application. The absoluteness of this position is inherently as dangerous as an earlier authority, as it soon can turn to coercion of the "scientific" perspective.

I have elaborated on Yan's perspective as representative of the dissidents not to critique the democracy movement, with which I am in sympathy, but to illustrate that there is no real evidence of any change regarding the bases of legitimation in Chinese political culture. The dissidents are as reliant on retelling the national myth and redefining ideological orthodoxy as are the leaders in Beijing. Were there to be a drastic reversal in the power relationships in China, it is reasonable to expect that the new regime would legitimate themselves much as previous regimes had done, and political structures would not likely be drastically altered. The most unfortunate implication of this contention is that if the "pillars" of legitimacy and governmental action remain the same, it is likely that governmental action itself will remain stable, preventing the free exchange of ideas and relying on coercion to attain governmental goals. As long as these two elements serve as the defining characteristics of political legitimation, we can expect their presence in any serious attempt at legitimation or delegitimation in Chinese politics and economics.

Another question we raised earlier relates to the ability of other nations to influence Chinese behavior, both internationally and domestically. The United States' attempts to alter China's domestic and foreign policy are perhaps the best well known, and serve as helpful examples. When the political and rhetorical impact of the national myth and ideology are considered, we see that many of these attempts are doomed from the start. Much of the early authority of the CCP was due to its clear stance opposing foreign intervention and control over China. The Treaty of Tianjin in 1858, the European colonialism of Chinese cities, and the Japanese invasion of China during the 1930s probably did more to guarantee victory for the CCP than did any of the Guomindang's corruption or decades of poverty.

Since the Party sprang from a nationalistic impulse, it is obvious that it would not benefit from reduced nationalistic sympathies. Mao Zedong suffered from Soviet involvement in the affairs of the Chinese Communist Party, and after he came to be chairman of the Party, unambiguously opposed Soviet intrusion into Chinese politics, allowing Soviet influence only so long as it helped his own position. Deng Xiaoping, while making openness to the outside world a definite policy, also has little patience for foreign "intrusion." In short, the national myth has little room for foreign involvement in domestic issues. This nationalistic impulse has been carefully cultivated, and there is no evidence that it is in any serious danger among China's younger generations.

Since this is the case, we can expect that any overt involvement in attempts to change China's political structure and policies will fail if they are perceived as foreign involvement. It is a fundamental tenet of the Chinese national myth to resist any foreign intrusion. While Western governments are likely to be embarrassed by international pressure and publicity, and thus are likely to compromise on sensitive political issues, Chinese leaders do not experience this pressure in the same way. It is more important to Western politicians to be a responsible member of the "international community" than to Chinese, who desire respect for Chinese sovereignty more than international community. Thus, international complaints of human rights abuses in China are likely to fall on deaf ears in Beijing.

This does not mean that all attempts to change China are doomed from the start. What it does suggest is that only efforts that conform to Chinese ideology and the national myth will be successful. The recent U.S. victory in gaining stronger enforcement of copyright law is successful largely because these were logical steps in China's economic growth. China would have eventually been internally motivated to take the same actions, such as strengthening copyright protection and protecting intellectual ownership, in order to encourage internal development of technology. U.S. threats to hurt the reform program itself by cutting off trade sealed the deal. It is not so clear that China is likely to be as persuaded by international outcry over human rights, concepts that only make sense in China when subsumed to the larger national myth. Deng Xiaoping is rumored to have said, "The most basic human right is the right to eat." In order to guarantee that right, it is legitimate to delay all others. As long as the myth of revolution and liberation remains in place, all attempts to improve human rights must be seen as consistent with that myth, rather than as foreign efforts to change China. Compromise is possible only insofar as it does not violate the national myth.

Conclusion

It has been my thesis that political discourse in China serves different political functions than it does in Western countries. Western politicians seek the approval of potential voters through discourse, and attempt to find language that "rings true" with the audience. Thus, they find themselves struggling to find policies they can reconcile with their language. Chinese political leaders attempt to find language that moves the public, and struggle to find language that reconciles their policies.

The current leaders remember the bitter sting of the Cultural Revolution, when reformist policies brought accusations of being counterrevolutionary, and many had ample opportunity in labor farms and prisons to contemplate the folly of their heterodoxy. Because the policies of moderation advocated by Deng and Chen Yun had no ideological (rhetorical) foundation equal to Mao's personal authority in the 1950s, and Deng and Chen had no mythic standing comparable to Mao's, their policies had no standing in the society. Deng and the reformers have learned these lessons well. By legitimating the reforms within the language of orthodox Marxism, the reformers protect themselves from the harsh winds that blow against heterodoxy.

But in a larger sense, the reforms themselves are an attempt to guard against the judgment of History. Deng Xiaoping and the reformers understand the technological and economic changes in the world, and are seeking to protect China's place in the world by not missing out on the greater turnings of history. Historical progression moves independent of China, and Deng and the reformers recognize that an unwavering commitment to Maoism will leave China at the tail end of the world's turnings.[18] To return to the historical analogy, China's leaders face a dilemma between loyalty to the current regime and loyalty to the Mandate of Heaven. Although, as Marxists, they view communism as the ultimate goal of history, it has become all too apparent that Marx's writings do not contain the answers to the questions posed by modernization. The technological and economic revolutions that have occurred, representing the Mandate, indicate that the ideological orthodoxy inherited from the first generation of revolutionaries is no longer adequate. It is this audience, History, that will judge the ultimate fruitfulness of any revolution.

Notes

Chapter One

1. X. L. Ding, *The Decline of Communism in China: Legitimacy Crisis, 1977-1989.* (New York: Cambridge University Press, 1994).

2. Peter M. Lichtenstein, *China at the Brink: The Political Economy of Reform and Retrenchment in the Post-Mao Era.* (New York: Praeger Press, 1991), 60.

3. Yan Jiaqi, *Toward a Democratic China.* (Honolulu: University of Hawaii Press, 1992), 101. Yan is actually quoting H. G. Wells.

4. Clifford Geertz, *The Interpretation of Cultures.* (New York: Basic Books, 1973), 5.

5. Godwin Chu, *Radical Change through Communication in China.* (Honolulu: East West Center, 1977), ix.

6. Harry Harding, *China's Second Revolution: Reform After Mao.* (Washington, D.C.: The Brookings Institution, 1977), 2.

7. Michael Schoenhals, *Doing Things with Words in Chinese Politics.* (Berkeley: Institute of East Asian Studies, 1992).

8. Schoenhals, 3.

9. Schoenhals, 20–21.

10. See for example, "On Literary Style," *Mao Tse-tung on Literature and Art.* (Beijing: Foreign Languages Press, 1977), 131.

11. Perry Link, *Evening Chats in Beijing.*(New York: W. W. Norton, 1992), 177.

12. Kenneth Burke, *A Rhetoric of Motives.* (Berkeley: University of California Press, 1969), 43.

13. Kenneth Burke, *A Grammar of Motives.* (Berkeley: University of California Press, 1969), 342.

14. Murray Edelman, *The Symbolic Uses of Politics*. (Urbana: University of Illinois Press, 1964), 18–19.

15. Donald N. McCloskey, *The Rhetoric of Economics*. (Madison, Wisconsin: The University of Wisconsin Press, 1985).

16. Schoenhals, 76.

17. Kenneth G. Lieberthal and Bruce J. Dickson, *A Research Guide to Central Party and Government Meetings in China, 1949–1986, rev. ed.* (London: M.E. Sharpe, 1989), xxii.

Chapter Two

1. Max Weber, *Economy and Society: An Outline of Interpretive Sociology*. (New York: Bedminster Press, 1968), 215; William Maley, "Political Legitimation in Contemporary Afghanistan," *Asian Survey* 27 (1987):705–25.

2. Jurgen Habermas, *Legitimation Crisis*. (Boston: Beacon Press, 1975); Robert Francesconi, "The Implications of Habermas' Theory of Legitimation for Rhetorical Criticism," *Communication Monographs* 53 (1986):16–35. See also Thomas Farrell, "Political Communication: Its Investigation and Praxis," *Western Speech Communication* 40 (1976):91–103.

3. Habermas, 101.

4. Habermas, 95.

5. Habermas, 110.

6. Habermas, 46.

7. Hok-lam Chan, for instance, argues that the rhetoric of legitimation in classical Chinese culture varies tremendously from that of other nations. See *Legitimation in Imperial China: Discussions under the Jurchen-Chin Dynasty.* (Seattle: University of Washington Press, 1984), especially pp. 42–48.

8. Habermas, 120

9. Habermas, 33. Habermas specifically says, "I must . . . limit myself to a *model* of the most important structural features of organized capitalism in order to derive from them the possible classes of crisis tendencies that *can* arise in this social formation. . . . It is not easy to determine empirically the probability of boundary conditions under which the *possible* crisis tendencies *actually* set in an prevail. The empirical indicators we have at our disposal are as yet inadequate." (Italics in original.)

10. Emile Sahliyeh, "Religious Resurgence and Political Moderniza-tion." In *Religious Resurgence and Politics in the Contemporary World*, Emile Sahliyeh, ed. (Albany: State University of New York Press, 1990), 16.

11. Robert Bellah, "Legitimation Processes in Politics and Religion," *Current Sociology* 35 (1987):89–99.

12. Donald C. Rice, *The Rhetorical Uses of the Authorizing Figure: Fidel Castro and José Martí*. (New York: Praeger, 1992).

13. D. Ray Heisey and J. David Trebing, "Authority and Legitimacy: A Rhetorical Case Study of the Iranian Revolution." *Communication Monographs*. 53 (1986):295–310.

14. Thomas Luckmann, "Comments on Legitimation," *Current Sociology* 35 (1987):109–117.

15. Luckmann, 111.

16. Luckmann, 110.

17. John Bryan Starr, *Ideology and Culture*. (New York: Harper and Row, 1973), 34–35.

18. Martha Solomon, "The Positive Woman's Journey: A Mythic Anal-ysis of the Rhetoric of Stop ERA," *Quarterly Journal of Speech* 65 (1979):262–74; Janice Hocker Rushing, "The Rhetoric of the American West-ern Myth," *Communication Monographs* 50 (1983):14–32; Farrel Corcoran, "The Bear in the Back Yard: Myth, Ideology, and Victimage Ritual in Soviet Funerals," *Communication Monographs* 50 (1983):305–320.

19. Jeff Bass and Richard Cherwitz have offered a similar understand-ing of political myth which they define as a "fusion of sacred myth and ide-ology."

20. Walter Fisher, *Human Communication as Narration: Toward a Philosophy of Reason, Value, and Action*. (Columbia, S.C.: University of South Carolina Press, 1987).

21. Anne Norton, *Reflections on Political Identity*. (Baltimore: Johns Hopkins University Press, 1988).

22. T. H. Rigby, "Introduction: Political Legitimacy, Weber, and Com-munist Mono-organizational Systems." In *Political Legitimation in Com-munist States*. T.H. Rigby and Ferenc Feher, eds. (New York: St. Martin's Press, 1982), 1–26. Rigby argues in particular that "the predominant orien-tation of [Soviet-type] command structures is towards goal-achievement, rather than towards the application of rules, which Weber correctly identi-fies as the predominant orientation of the public bureaucracies of Western

'capitalist' systems . . . [consequently,] the legitimacy claimed for the commands issuing from this system and for those holding office under it is framed in terms of 'goal-rationality' rather than the formal-legal rationality of Western 'capitalist' systems."

23. Rigby, 14.

24. Luckmann, 112.

25. This view accords with Walter Fisher, "A Motive View of Communication," *Quarterly Journal of Speech* 56 (1970):131–139.

26. Steven Sangren, *History and Magical Power in a Chinese Community.* (Stanford: Stanford University Press, 1987), 3.

27. Mao Zedong, "The May 4th Movement." In *The Selected Works of Mao Tse-tung*, vol. 2. (Beijing: Foreign Language Press, 1975), 237.

28. Steven Sangren, "History and the Rhetoric of Legitimacy: The Matsu Cult of Taiwan," *Comparative Studies in Society and History* 30 (1988), 677.

29. Sangren, *History and Magical Power*, 166.

30. Kenneth Burke, *The Rhetoric of Religion.* (Boston: Beacon Press, 1961), 307.

31. Sangren "History and the Rhetoric of Legitimacy" 687–88.

32. For a discussion of the role of pre-Republican values on contemporary Chinese society, see Steven Chafee and Godwin Chu, "Communication and Cultural Change in China," in *Comparatively Speaking: Communication and Culture across Space and Time*, eds. Jay G. Blumler, Jack M. McLeod, and Karl Erik Rosengren, eds. (Beverly Hills: Sage, 1992), 209–237.

33. Simon Leys, *The Emperors New Clothes.* (London: Allison and Busby, 1981), 232.

34. Lucian Pye, *Asian Power and Politics.* (Cambridge, Mass.: Harvard University Press, 1985), 185.

35. Pye, *Asian Power*, 185.

36. Mao "Orientation of the Youth Movement," 245.

37. Maurice Meisner, *Mao's China and After.* (New York: Free Press, 1986), 17.

38. William F. Dorrill, "Transfer of Legitimacy in the Chinese Communist Party: Origins of the Maoist Myth." In *Party Leadership and Revo-*

lutionary Power in China. John Wilson Lewis, ed. (Cambridge: Cambridge University Press, 1970), 69. Helmut Martin argues that the 1945 Resolution represented Mao's own view of the Party's history. See Helmut Martin, *Cult and Canon: The Origins and Development of State Maoism.* (Armonk, N.Y.: M. E. Sharpe, 1982), 9.

39. Dorrill, 85.

40. Dorrill, 112.

41. Dorrill, 112.

42. Frederick C. Teiwes, *Leadership, Legitimacy, and Conflict in China.* (Armonk, N.Y.: M. E. Sharpe, 1984).

43. Privately, some Chinese argue that Peng's downfall was due to his failure to adequately protect Mao's only son from American bombs during the Korean War, leading to the younger Mao's death.

44. *Peking Review*, April 22, 1966:22–24.

45. For a compendium of the what is called the "devotional literature" surrounding Mao, see *The Miracles of Chairman Mao.* George Urban, ed. (London: Tom Stacey, 1971).

46. Teiwes, 43.

47. Jung Chang, *Wild Swans: Three Daughters of China.* (New York: Anchor/Doubleday, 1992), 262.

48. Quoted in Martin, 15.

49. Chang, 262.

50. Hok-lam Chan, 24.

51. Wing-tsit Chan, *Sourcebook in Chinese Philosophy.* (Princeton: Princeton University Press, 1963), 6–7.

52. Lance Eccles, "The Seizure of the Mandate: Establishment of the Legitimacy of the Liang Dynasty," *Journal of Asian History*, 23 (1989):176.

53. Sangren, "History and the Rhetoric of Legitimacy," 688.

54. Teiwes, 61.

55. Yan Jiaqi, *Toward a Democratic China.* (Honolulu: University of Hawaii Press, 1992), 109–110.

56. Sangren, "History and the Rhetoric of Legitimacy," 689.

57. Starr, 35.

58. Lucian W. Pye, *Asian Power and Politics*. (Cambridge, Mass.: Harvard University Press, 1985) 182–83.

59. Mao, "Orientation of the Youth Movement" *The Selected Works of Mao Tse-tung*. vol. 2 (Beijing: Foreign Language Press, 1965), 243.

60. Mao, "The May 4th Movement," 238.

61. Benjamin I. Schwartz, "The Reign of Virtue: Some Broad Perspectives on Leader and Party in the Cultural Revolution." In *Party Leadership and Revolutionary Power in China*, John Wilson Lewis, ed. (New York: Cambridge University Press, 1970), 157.

62. Ram Naresh Sharma, "Mao's Concepts of Power, Authority, and Legitimacy," *China Report* 25 (1989):135–45. Although the CCP would acknowledge the possibility of someone from outside the proletariat being orthodox, such as Chairman Mao's background as a rich peasant, the experience of the Rectification Movement and the Cultural Revolution demonstrates the conviction that this possibility is only fulfilled in rare instances.

63. William R. Brown, "Ideology as Communication Process," *Quarterly Journal of Speech* 64 (1978):123–40.

64. Harry Harding, *China's Second Revolution: Reform after Mao*. (Washington, D.C.: The Brookings Institution, 1987), 289.

65. Pye, *Asian Power*, 187.

66. Norton, 70.

67. Liu Binyan, *Tell the Truth*. (New York: Pantheon Books, 1989), 80.

68. Hua Guofeng, "Political Report to the Eleventh National Congress of the Communist Party of China," *Documents of the Eleventh National Congress of the Communist Party of China*. (Beijing: Foreign Language Press, 1977), 109.

69. Deng Xiaoping, "The Organizational Line Guarantees the Implementation of the Ideological and Political Lines," *The Selected Works of Deng Xiaoping*. (Beijing, Foreign Language Press, 1984), 291.

70. Yan, 211–12.

71. Lucien Pye, *The Spirit of Chinese Politics*, 2nd ed. (Cambridge, Mass.: Harvard University Press, 1992), 16.

72. Pye, *Spirit*, 31.

73. Pye, *Asian Power*, 186.

74. Martin, 4.

75. *The Selected Works of Mao Zedong*. (5 vols.) (Beijing: Foreign Language Press, 1976).

76. Edgar Snow, *Red China Today*. (New York: Vintage, 1970), 100.

77. Mao Zedong, "Be Concerned with the Well-Being of the Masses, Pay Attention to Methods of Work," in *The Selected Works of Mao Tse-tung*. vol. 1 (Beijing: Foreign Language Press, 1965), 151.

78. Ralph Thaxton, *China Turned Rightside Up: Revolutionary Legitimacy in the Peasant World*. (New Haven: Yale University Press, 1983), 220.

79. Mao, "Orientation of the Youth Movement," 246.

80. Schwartz, 157.

81. *Beijing Review*, 29 October 1976:13; cited in Stephen Uhalley, Jr., *A History of the Chinese Communist Party*. (Stanford: Hoover Institution Press, 1988) 186.

82. Benjamin I. Schwartz, *Communism and China: Ideology in Flux*. (Cambridge, Mass.: Harvard University Press, 1968), 34.

Chapter Three

1. Edward Friedman, "Reconstructing China's National Identity: A Southern Alternative to Mao-Era Anti-Imperialist Nationalism," *Journal of Asian Studies* 53, 1 (February, 1994):67–91.

2. Maurice Meisner, *Mao's China and After*. (New York: Free Press, 1986), 448. *Ni ban shi, wo fang xin*. Although the scrap of paper on which Mao's note appeared was constantly reproduced in the press, there is some doubt as to its authenticity.

3. Frederick Wakeman, "Revolutionary Rites: The Remains of Chiang Kai-shek and Mao Tse-tung," *Representations* 10 (1985):167–68.

4. Maurice Meisner, *Mao's China and After*. (New York: Free Press, 1986), 462.

5. Jonathan Spence, *The Search for Modern China*. (New York: W. W. Norton, 1990), 648–49.

6. Wakeman, 152.

7. David Chang, *Zhou Enlai and Deng Xiaopeng in the Chinese Leadership Succession Crisis*. (Lanham, Md.: University Press of America, 1984), 179.

8. Harrison E. Salisbury, *The New Emperors: China in the Era of Mao and Deng*. (Boston: Little, Brown, 1992), 378.

9. Stuart R. Schram, "'Economics in Command?' Ideology and Policy since the Third Plenum, 1978–84," *China Quarterly* 99 (1984):419.

10. Hsi-sheng Ch'i, *Politics of Disillusionment: The Chinese Communist Party Under Deng Xiaopeng, 1978–89*. (Armonk, N.Y.: M. E. Sharpe, 1991), 4–5.

11. For an analysis of this period, see Ch'i.

12. Lucian Pye, *The Spirit of Chinese Politics*, 2nd ed. (Cambridge, Mass.: Harvard University Press, 1992).

13. Pye, 6.

14. Lowell Dittmer, "Ideology and Organization in Post-Mao China," *Asian Survey* 24 (1984):355.

15. *The Resolution on CPC History*. (Beijing: Foreign Language Press, 1981), 49. Hereafter referred to as *Resolution*.

16. Kenneth G. Lieberthal and Bruce J. Dickson, *A Research Guide to Central Party and Government Meetings in China:1949–1986*. (Armonke, N.Y.: M.E. Sharpe, 1989), 259. "Third Party Plenum Communique Discussed Throughout Country," Foreign Broadcast Information Service-China, 28 December 1978:E1. The full text of the Communique is reprinted in *Peking Review*, 29 December 1978:6–16.

17. Hua Guofeng, "Political Report to the Eleventh National Congress of the Communist Party of China," *Documents of the Eleventh National Congress of the Communist Party of China*. (Beijing: Foreign Language Press, 1977), 53.

18. "Communique of the Third Plenary Session of the Eleventh Central Committee of the Communist Party of China," *Peking Review*, 29 December 1978:9–11. Hereafter referred to as "Communique."

19. "Communique," 10.

20. "Communique," 11.

21. "Communique," 16.

22. "Communique," 15.

23. "Communique," 15.

24. Deng Xiaoping, "The 'Two Whatevers' Do Not Accord with Marxism," in *Selected Works of Deng Xiaoping.* (Beijing: Foreign Language Press, 1984), 51.

25. "Communique," 13.

26. "Communique," 13.

27. "Communique," 13–14.

28. "Communique," 11.

29. "Communique," 14.

30. "Communique," 15.

31. "Communique," 15.

32. Foreign Broadcast Information Service-CHINA, 28 December 1978:E3.

33. Foreign Broadcast Information Service-CHINA, 28 December 1978:E1.

34. Wakeman, 160.

35. Byron S. J. Weng, Introduction. In *Mao Zedong: A Preliminary Reassessment*, Stuart Schram, ed. (Hong Kong: Chinese University Press, 1983), viii.

36. Deng, 284–85.

37. James T. Myers, "Whatever Happened to Chairman Mao?: Myth and Charisma in the Chinese Revolution." In *Chinese Politics from Mao to Deng*, Victor C. Falkenheim, ed. (New York: Paragon Press, 1989), 30.

38. Meisner, 458.

39. Andrew J. Nathan, *Chinese Democracy.* (Berkeley: University of California Press, 1985), 7.

40. Meisner, 461.

41. Foreign Broadcast Information Service-CHINA, 30 June 1981:K2–K4.

42. "Communique," 15.

43. *Resolution*, 33.

44. John Gardner, *Chinese Politics and the Succession to Mao.* (New York: Holmes and Meier, 1982), 194.

45. *Resolution*, 42–43.

46. *Resolution*, 72–73.

47. Helmut Martin, *Cult and Canon: The Origins and Development of State Maoism.* (Armonk, N.Y.: M. E. Sharpe, 1982), 15.

48. George Urban, ed., *The Miracles of Chairman Mao.* (London: Tom Stacey, 1971).

49. Quoted in Wakeman, 166.

50. Stuart Schram, *Mao Zedong: A Preliminary Reassessment.* (Hong Kong: Chinese University Press, 1983), 84.

51. Schram, 84.

52. *Resolution*, 56.

53. *Resolution*, 68.

54. *Resolution*, 70.

55. Jung Chang, *Wild Swans: Three Daughters of China.* (New York: Anchor/Doubleday, 1992), 262.

56. Gardner, 193.

57. David Bonavia, "How History Was Revised: Hua Reviled, Hu Revived," *Far Eastern Economic Review*, 10 September 1982:14.

58. Deng Xiaoping, "Opening Speech," in *The Twelfth National Congress of the CPC.* (Beijing: Foreign Language Press, 1982), 3.

59. Stephen Uhalley, Jr., *A History of the Chinese Communist Party.* (Stanford: Hoover Institution Press, 1988), 58.

60. Deng Xiaoping, *Building Socialism with Chinese Characteristics.* (Beijing: Foreign Language Press, 1984.)

61. Hu Yaobang, "Create a New Situation in All Fields of Socialist Modernization," in *The Twelfth National Congress of the CPC.* (Beijing: Foreign Language Press, 1982), 17.

62. Hu, 12.

63. Hu, 10.

64. Hu, 11.

65. Stuart R. Schram, "'Economics in Command?' Ideology and Policy Since the Third Plenum, 1978–84." *China Quarterly* 99 (1984):431–33.

66. Schram, "'Economics in Command,'" 433.

67. Schram, "'Economics in Command,'" 433.

68. Hu, 43–44.

69. Hu, 64.

70. Hu, 80.

71. Hu, 83.

72. Cited in Feng Jicai, *Voices from the Whirlwind: An Oral History of the Chinese Cultural Revolution.* (New York: Pantheon Press, 1991), 105.

Chapter Four

1. William Safire, "Greatest Leap Forward," *New York Times*, 10 December 1984; cited in Harry Harding, *China's Second Revolution: Reform after Mao.* (Washington, D.C.: The Brookings Institution, 1987), 128.

2. *Time*, vol. 113, 1, 1 January 1979; vol. 127, 1, 6 January 1986.

3. Sophie Quinn-Judge, "A model for reform: China's example inspires Soviet reformers," *Far Eastern Economic Review*, 25 May 1989:16.

4. Carol Hamrin, *China and the Challenge of the Future.* (Boulder, Colo.: Westview Press, 1990), 159.

5. An-chia Wu, "The 'Initial Stage of Socialism': Background, Tasks, and Impact." In *Mainland China after the Thirteenth Party Congress*, King-yuh Chang, ed. (Boulder, Colo.: Westview Press, 1990), 30. See also Kai Ma, "The Dilemma Facing Economic Reform in Mainland China." In *Mainland China after the Thirteenth Party Congress*. King-yuh Chang, ed. (Boulder, Colo.: Westview Press, 1990), 403.

6. Wu, 32

7. John P. Burns and Stanley Rosen, eds. *Policy Conflicts in Post-Mao China: A Documentary Survey, with Analysis.* (Armonk, N.Y.: M. E. Sharpe, 1986), 1.

8. Harding, 100.

9. Jonathan Spence, *The Search for Modern China.* (New York: W. W. Norton, 1990), 719.

10. Spence, 719.

11. Lucien Pye, *The Spirit of Chinese Politics*, 2nd ed. (Cambridge, Mass.: Harvard University Press, 1992), 12–16.

12. Cited in Geremie Barmé and John Minford, eds. *Seeds of Fire: Chinese Voices of Conscience*. (Hong Kong: Far Eastern Economic Review Press, 1986), 271.

13. *New York Times*, 3 January 1987. Cited by Spence, 725.

14. Zhao Ziyang, "Advance Along the Road of Socialism with Chinese Characteristics," *Documents of the Thirteenth National Congress of the Communist Party of China (1987)*. (Beijing: Foreign Language Press, 1987), 9.

15. Zhao, 5.

16. Wu, 32

17. Zhao, 10.

18. Zhao, 12.

19. Zhao, 5.

20. Zhao, 8.

21. Zhao, 9.

22. Zhao, 8.

23. Mao Zedong, "On Contradiction" *Selected Works of Mao Tsetung*. vol. 1 (Beijing: Foreign Language Press, 1965), 311–347.

24. Zhao, 12–13.

25. Zhao, 14.

26. Zhao, 32.

27. Zhao, 42.

28. Zhao, 42.

29. Zhao, 46.

30. Zhao, 69.

31. Zhao, 69.

32. Zhao, 77.

33. Wu, 40–41.

34. *The 13th Party Congress and China's Reforms.* (Beijing: Beijing Review Press, 1987), 8.

35. *The Thirteenth Party Congress and China's Reforms,* 13.

36. Willy Wo-lap Lam, *The Era of Zhao Ziyang: Power Struggle in China, 1986–88.* (Hong Kong: A. B. Books and Stationary (International), 1989), 200.

37. Lam, 201.

38. Lam, 201.

39. Feng-hwa Mah, "'Primary Stage,' Leasing, and Ownership: Mainland Chinese Economy at the Crossroads," *Mainland China after the Thirteenth Party Congress,* King-yuh Chang, ed. (Boulder, Colo.: Westview Press, 1990), 339–358.

40. King-yuh Chang, ed. *Mainland China after the Thirteenth Party Congress.* (Boulder, Colo.: Westview Press, 1990), 2.

Chapter Five

1. Roderick MacFarquhar, "Deng's last campaign," *New York Review of Books,* vol. xxxix (21), 17 December 1992:22.

2. In recent Chinese politics, "right" usually refers to the more liberal elements within the society, including many intellectuals and democracy advocates, while "left" refers to the conservative, Maoist segments of the society. For an analysis on some of the theoretical debate surrounding the reforms, see Luo Man, "Another Wave of Debate on Economic Theory," *China Market* 1 (1991):10–11.

3. Peter M. Lichtenstein, *China at the Brink: The Political Economy of Reform and Retrenchment in the Post-Mao Era.* (New York: Praeger Press, 1991) 78–79.

4. Lichtenstein, 79.

5. Willy Wo-lap Lam, *The Era of Zhao Ziyang: Power Struggle in China, 1986–88.* (Hong Kong: A. B. Books and Stationary (International), 1989), 265.

6. Yan Jiaqi, *Toward a Democratic China.* (Honolulu: University of Hawaii Press, 1992) 151–52.

7. See, for example, Lam, cited above.

8. Lam, 265–56.

9. Sophie Quinn-Judge, "A model for reform," *Far Eastern Economic Review*, 25 May 1989:16.

10. Michael Parks, "Soviets still socialistic, China's Premier says." *Los Angeles Times*, 26 April 1990:A4.

11. David Holley, "Beijing outlines policy to stay on socialist path," *Los Angeles Times*, 5 Mar. 1990:A5.

12. Stanley Rosen, "The Effect of Post-June 4 Reeducation Campaigns on Chinese Students," *China Quarterly* 134, June 1993:310–25.

13. Li Changjiu, "Objectively Understand Modern Capitalism," *Guangming Ribao*, 23 July 1992:3, cited in Foreign Broadcast Information Service-CHINA, 92–165, 25 August 1992:40.

14. Liu Binyan, *Tell the Truth* (New York: Pantheon Books, 1989), 6.

15. Yan, 152

16. Jonathan Spence, *The Search for Modern China*. (New York: W. W. Norton, 1990), 742.

17. Han Minzhu, ed. *Cries for Democracy: Writings and Speeches from the 1989 Chinese Democracy Movement*. (Princeton: Princeton University Press, 1990), 6.

18. "Reflections on the History of the Chinese Communist Party," Han Minzhu, 59–60.

19. Liu, 37–38.

20. Liu, 43.

21. See, for example, *Cries for Democracy: Writings and Speeches from the 1989 Chinese Democracy Movement*, ed. Han Minzhu (Princeton: Princeton University Press, 1990). For an account of the events from the government's perspective, see *The Truth about the Beijing Turmoil* (Beijing: Beijing Publishing House, 1989).

22. "Deng Xiaoping's Remarks to Martial Law Officers on June 9," in Han Minzhu, 369–70.

23. "New May Fourth Manifesto," Han Minzhu, 135.

24. "Urgent Call to Mobilize from the Protect Tiananmen Headquarters," Han Minzhu, 359.

25. Yan, 160–61.

26. Lincoln Kaye, "Deng Speaks Out," *Far Eastern Economic Review*, 13 February 1992:10.

27. Jiang Zemin, "Accelerating Reform and Opening-Up," *Beijing Review*, 26 October–1 November 1992:10–33.

28. Jiang, 10–11.

29. Jiang, 10–11.

30. Jiang, 11.

31. Jiang, 11.

32. Jiang, 29.

33. Jiang, 14.

34. Jiang, 15.

35. Jiang, 33.

36. Jiang, 15.

37. Jiang, 15.

38. Jiang, 16.

39. Jiang, 18.

40. Jiang, 18.

41. Jiang, 20

42. Jiang, 16.

43. Jiang, 16.

44. Jiang, 17.

45. Jiang, 25.

46. Jiang, 30.

47. Geng Yuxin, "China Turns to Market Economy," *Beijing Review*, 9–15 November 1992:7.

48. David Holley, "China's new leaders get a blessing from Deng," *Los Angeles Times*, 20 October 1992:A4.

49. Sandra Henry, "Deng Xiaoping Triumphs," *China Trade Report*, November 1992 (30):1.

50. Willy Wo-lap Lam, "[Deng] fears 'roll back' of reforms," *South China Morning Post*, 19 January 1993:8. Cited in Foreign Broadcast Information Service-China, 93-011, 19 January 1993:20.

51. David Holley, "China to ratify basis for market reforms," *Los Angeles Times*, 16 February 1992:A22.

52. Stanley Rosen, "Students and the State in China: The Crisis in Ideology and Organization." In *State and Society in China: The Consequences of Reform*, Arthur Lewis Rosenbaum, ed. (Boulder: Westview Press, 1992), 167.

53. M. Whyte, "The Social Sources of the Student Demonstrations." In *China Briefing: 1990*, A. J. Kane, ed. (Boulder: Westview Press, 1990), 47–63.

54. Liu, 33.

55. "Beijing Reaffirms Stance That Zhao Erred in Uprising," *Los Angeles Times* 10 October 1992:A1.

56. Li Haibo, "The Man Who Makes History," *Beijing Review*, 12–18 October 1992:13.

57. "Deng refuses formulation of 'Deng Xiaoping Thought," *Ching Pao* (Hong Kong), 5 October 1992:43. Cited in Foreign Broadcast Information Service-CHINA 92–195, 7 October 1992:13.

58. New York: Basic Books, 1995. Originally published as *Wo de fuqin Deng Xiaoping* (Beijing: Zhongyang Wenxiang Publishing House, 1993).

Chapter Six

1. Wing-tsit Chan, *A Sourcebook in Chinese Philosophy*. (Princeton: Princeton University Press, 1969), 40.

2. Robert Oliver, *Communication and Culture in Ancient China and India*. (Syracuse, N.Y.: Syracuse University Press, 1971), 10.

3. Deng Maomao, *My Father Deng Xiaoping*. (New York: Basic Books, 1995). Originally published as *Wo de fuqin Deng Xiaoping* (Beijing: Zhongyang Wenxiang Publishing House, 1993).

4. Li Haibo, "The Man Who Makes History," *Beijing Review*, 12–18 October 1992:13.

5. Robert Bellah, "Legitimation Processes in Politics and Religion," *Current Sociology* 35, 2 (1987):89–99.

6. Merle Goldman, *China's Intellectuals: Advise and Dissent.* (Cambridge, Mass.: Harvard University Press, 1981), 32–36.

7. Harrison Salisbury, *The New Emperors: China in the Era of Mao and Deng.* (Boston: Little, Brown, 1992). Although it is true that Mao actively encouraged the personality cult that achieved godlike proportions, especially in his later years, his motives for this are far from clear. It is evident that Deng has personally rejected such a cult and in recent years has repeatedly attempted to establish procedural rules to eliminate the possibility of future emperors.

8. Walter Fisher, *Human Communication as Narration: Toward a Philosophy of Reason, Value, and Action.* (Columbia, S.C.: University of South Carolina Press, 1987).

9. Lucian Pye, *The Dynamics of Chinese Politics.* (Cambridge, Mass.: Oelgeschlager, Gunn & Hain, 1981), 167–69.

10. An example of this is the National People's Congress revision of Li Peng's report to the Congress, in which Li's speech was revised to include greater references to the reformist rhetoric. See David Holley, "Doubt cast on Chinese leader's future." *Los Angeles Times,* 4 April 1992.

11. Pye, 167–69.

12. Alan P. L. Liu, *How China Is Ruled.* (Englewood Cliffs, N.J.: Prentice-Hall, 1986), 264.

13. Perry Link, *Evening Chats in Beijing.* (New York: W. W. Norton, 1992), 177.

14. "Deng Xiaoping's remarks to martial law officers on June 9," in *Cries for Democracy,* 370.

15. David Holley, "Power in Beijing finally flowing to younger generation," *Los Angeles Times,* 2 April 1993:A8.

16. "Religion, Reason, and Practice: Visits to Three Courts of Law," in Yan Jiaqi, *Towards a Democratic China: The Intellectual Autobiography of Yan Jiaqi.* (Honolulu: School of Hawaiian Asian and Pacific Studies, University of Hawaii, 1992) 165–90.

17. Yan Jiaqi, "My Four Convictions Regarding Science." In *Towards a Democratic China: The Intellectual Autobiography of Yan Jiaqi,* Yan Jiaqi, ed., 211–213.

18. Deng has openly identified himself as a pragmatist, as opposed to a dogmatic Marxist. For a revealing glimpse of Deng's attitudes toward Marxism in general, see FBIS-CHINA, 92–195, 7 October 1992:13.

Works Cited

Barmé, Geremie, and John Minford, eds. *Seeds of Fire: Chinese Voices of Conscience*. Hong Kong: Far Eastern Economic Review Press, 1986.

Bass, Jeff D., and Richard Cherwitz. "Imperial Mission and Manifest Destiny: A Case Study of Political Myth in Rhetorical Discourse." *Southern Speech Communication Journal* 43 (1978):213–32.

Beijing Review, 29 October 1976.

Bellah, Robert, "Legitimation Processes in Politics and Religion." *Current Sociology* 35 (1987):89–99.

Bernstein, Thomas P. "Ideology and Rural Reform: The Paradox of Contingent Stability."In *State and Society in China: The Consequences of Reform*, Arthur Lewis Rosenbaum, ed. Boulder, Colo.: Westview Press, 1992.

Bonavia, David. "How History Was Revised: Hua Reviled, Hu Revived." *Far Eastern Economic Review*, 10 September 1982:14 .

Breen, Miles, and Farrel Corcoran. "Myth in the Television Discourse." *Communication Monographs* 49 (1982):127–136.

Brown, William R. "Ideology as Communication Process." *Quarterly Journal of Speech* 64 (1978):123–40.

Burke, Kenneth. *Counterstatement*. Berkeley: University of California Press, 1968.

———. *A Grammar of Motives*. Berkeley: University of California Press, 1969.

———. *A Rhetoric of Motives*. Berkeley: University of California Press, 1969.

———. *The Rhetoric of Religion*. Boston: Beacon Press, 1961.

Burns, John P., and Stanley Rosen, eds. *Policy Ccnflicts in Post-Mao China: A Documentary Survey, with Analysis*. Armonk, N.Y.: M. E. Sharpe, 1986.

Chafee, Steven, and Godwin Chu. "Communication and Cultural Change in China." In *Comparatively Speaking: Communication and Culture across Space and Time*, Jay G. Blumler, Jack M. McLeod, and Karl Erik Rosengren, eds. Beverly Hills: Sage, 1992, 209–237.

Chan, Hok-lam. *Legitimation in Imperial China: Discussions under the Jurchen-Chin Dynasty*. Seattle: University of Washington Press, 1984.

Chan, Wing-tsit, ed. *Sourcebook in Chinese Philosophy*. Princeton: Princeton University Press, 1963.

Chang, David. *Zhou Enlai and Deng Xiaopeng in the Chinese Leadership Succession Crisis*. Lanham, Md.: University Press of America, 1984.

Chang, David Wen-Wei. *China under Deng Xiaoping*. London: Macmillan Press, 1988.

Chang, Jung. *Wild Swans: Three Daughters of China*. New York: Anchor/Doubleday, 1992.

Chang, King-yuh. "Introduction." In *Mainland China after the Thirteenth Party Congress*, King-yuh Chang, ed. Boulder, Colo.: Westview Press, 1990.

Ch'i, Hsi-sheng. *Politics of Disillusionment: The Chinese Communist Party under Deng Xiaoping, 1978–89*. London: M.E. Sharpe, 1991.

Chu, Godwin. *Radical Change through Communication in China*. Honolulu: East West Center, 1977.

Collins, Catherine Ann, and Jeanne E. Clark, "Jim Wright's Resignation Speech: De-Legitimization or Redemption?" *Southern Communication Journal* 58, 1 (1992):67–75.

"Communique of the Third Plenary Session of the Eleventh Central Committee of the Communist Party of China." *Peking Review* 29 December 1978:9–11.

Condit, Celeste Michelle. "Post-Burke: Transcending the Sub-stance of Dramatism." *Quarterly Journal of Speech* 78 (1992): 339–355.

Corcoran, Farrel. "The Bear in the Back Yard: Myth, Ideology, and Victimage Ritual in Soviet Funerals." *Communication Monographs* 50 (1983):305–320.

Cushman, Donald P. "Contemporary Chinese Philosophy and Political Communication." In *Communication Theory: Eastern and Western Perspectives*, D. Lawrence Kincaid, ed. New York: Academic Press, 1987.

Deng Xiaoping. *Selected Works of Deng Xiaoping*. Beijing: Foreign Language Press, 1984.

Deng Xiaoping, "Opening Speech." *The Twelfth National Congress of the CPC*. Beijing: Foreign Language Press, 1982.

Dittmer, Lowell. "Ideology and Organization in Post-Mao China." *Asian Survey* 24 (1984):355.

Dorrill, William F. "Transfer of Legitimacy in the Chinese Communist Party: Origins of the Maoist Myth." In *Party Leadership and Revolutionary Power in China*, John Wilson Lewis, ed. Cambridge: Cambridge University Press, 1970.

Eccles, Lance. "The Seizure of the Mandate: Establishment of the Legitimacy of the Liang Dynasty." *Journal of Asian History* 23 (1989).

Edelman, Murray. *The Symbolic Uses of Politics*. Urbana: University of Illinois Press, 1964.

Falkenheim, Victor C., ed. *Chinese Politics from Mao to Deng*. New York: Paragon Press, 1989.

Farrell, Thomas. "Knowledge, Consensus, and Rhetorical Theory." *Quarterly Journal of Speech* 62 (1976):1–14.

――――. "Political Communication: Its Investigation and Praxis." *Western Speech Communication* 40 (1976):91–103.

Fisher, Walter. "A Motive View of Communication." *Quarterly Journal of Speech* 56 (1970):131–139.

――――. *Human Communication as Narration: Toward a Philosophy of Reason, Value, and Action*. Columbia, S.C.: University of South Carolina Press, 1987.

Francesconi, Robert. "James Hunt, The Wilmington 10, and Institutional Legitimacy." *Quarterly Journal of Speech* 68 (1982):47–59.

――――. "The Implications of Habermas' Theory of Legitimation for Rhetorical Criticism." *Communication Monographs* 53 (1986):16–35.

Gardner, John. *Chinese Politics and the Succession to Mao*. New York: Holmes and Meier, 1982.

Geng Yuxin. "China Turns to Market Economy." *Beijing Review*, 9–15 November 1992:7.

Goldman, Merle. *Chinese Intellectuals: Advise and Dissent*. Cambridge, Mass.: Harvard University Press, 1981.

Habermas, Jurgen. *Communication and the Evolution of Society*. Boston, Mass.: Beacon Press, 1979.

―――. *Legitimation Crisis*. Boston, Mass.: Beacon Press, 1975.

Hamrin, Carol. *China and the Challenge of the Future*. Boulder, Colo.: Westview Press, 1990.

Harding, Harry. *China's Second Revolution: Reform after Mao*. Washington, D.C.: The Brookings Institution, 1987.

Heisey, D. Ray, and J. David Trebing. "Authority and Legitimacy: A Rhetorical Case Study of the Iranian Revolution." *Communication Monographs* 53 (1986):295–310.

Henry, Sandra. "Deng Xiaoping Triumphs." *China Trade Report* 30 (1992):1.

Holley, David. "Beijing outlines policy to stay on socialist path." *Los Angeles Times*, 5 March 1990:A5.

Holley, David. "China's new leaders get a blessing from Deng." *Los Angeles Times*, 20 October 1992:A4.

Hu Yaobang. "Create a New Situation in All Fields of Socialist Modernization." *The Twelfth National Congress of the CPC*. Beijing: Foreign Language Press, 1982.

Hua Guofeng. "Political Report to the Eleventh National Congress of the Communist Party of China." *Documents of the Eleventh National Congress of the Communist Party of China*. Beijing: Foreign Language Press, 1977.

Jiang Zemin. "Accelerating Reform and Opening-Up." *Beijing Review*, 26 October–1 November 1992:10–33.

Kai Ma, "The Dilemma Facing Economic Reform in Mainland China." In *Mainland China after the Thirteenth Party Congress*. Kingyuh Chang, ed. Boulder, Colo.: Westview Press, 1990.

Kaye, Lincoln. "Deng Speaks Out." *Far Eastern Economic Review*, 13 February 1992:10.

Kristof, Nicholas D. "Now Tiger of Tiananmen Is Wounded." *New York Times*, 25 March 1992:A4.

Lam, Willy Wo-lap. *The Era of Zhao Ziyang: Power Struggle in China, 1986–88*. Hong Kong: A. B. Books and Stationary (International), 1989.

Leys, Simon. *The Emperors New Clothes*. London: Allison and Busby, 1981.

Lichtenstein, Peter M. *China at the Brink: The Political Economy of Reform and Retrenchment in the Post-Mao Era.* New York: Praeger Press, 1991.

Lieberthal, Kenneth G., and Bruce J. Dickson. *A Research Guide to Central Party and Government Meetings in China, 1949–1986,* rev. ed. London: M.E. Sharpe, 1989.

Liu, Alan P. L. *How China Is Ruled.* Englewood Cliffs, N.J.: Prentice-Hall, 1986.

Liu Binyan. *Tell the Truth.* New York: Pantheon Books, 1989.

Luckmann, Thomas. "Comments on Legitimation." *Current Sociology* 35 (1987):109–117.

Ma, Feng-hwa. "'Primary Stage,' Leasing, and Ownership: Mainland Chinese Economy at the Crossroads." In *Mainland China after the Thirteenth Party Congress,* King-yuh Changk, ed. Boulder, Colo.: Westview Press, 1990:339–58.

Macfarquhar, Roderick. "Deng's Last Campaign." *New York Review of Books,* vol xxxix (21), 17 December 1992.

Maley, William. "Political Legitimation in Contemporary Afghanistan." *Asian Survey* 27 (1987):705–25.

Mao Zedong. *Mao Tse-tung on Literature and Art.* Beijing: Foreign Languages Press, 1977.

———. *The Selected Works of Mao Tse-tung,* 5 vols. Beijing: Foreign Language Press, 1976.

Martin, Helmut. *Cult and Canon: The Origins and Development of State Maoism.* Armonk, N.Y.: M. E. Sharpe, 1982.

McCloskey, Donald N. *The Rhetoric of Economics.* Madison: The University of Wisconsin Press, 1985.

Meisner, Maurice. *Mao's China and After.* New York: Free Press, 1986.

Myers, James T. "Whatever Happened to Chairman Mao?: Myth and Charisma in the Chinese Revolution." In *Chinese Politics from Mao to Deng.* Victor C. Falkenheim, ed. New York: Paragon Press, 1989:17–40.

Nathan, Andrew J. *Chinese Democracy.* Berkeley: University of California Press, 1985.

Oliver, Robert. *Communication and Culture in Ancient China and India.* Syracuse, N.Y.: Syracuse University Press, 1971.

Parks, Michael. "Soviets still socialistic, China's Premier says." *Los Angeles Times*. 26 April 1990:A4.

Peking Review, 22 April 1966:22–24.

Peking Review, 29 December 1978:6–16.

Pye, Lucian. *The Dynamics of Chinese Politics*. Cambridge, Mass.: Oelgeschlager, Gunn and Hain, 1981.

——— . *Asian Power and Politics*. Cambridge, Mass.: Harvard University Press, 1985.

——— . *The Spirit of Chinese Politics*, new edition. Cambridge, Mass.: Harvard University Press, 1992.

Quinn-Judge, Sophie. "A Model for Reform: China's Example Inspires Soviet Reformers." *Far Eastern Economic Review*, 25 May 1989:16.

"Reflections on the History of the Chinese Communist Party." In *Cries for Democracy: Writings and Speeches from the 1989 Chinese Democracy Movement*, Han Minzhu, ed. Princeton: Princeton University Press, 1990, 59–60.

Resolution on CPC History. Beijing: Foreign Language Press, 1981.

Reynolds, Beatrice K. "Mao Tse-tung: Rhetoric of a Revolutionary." *Central States Speech Journal* 27 (1976):212–17.

Rice, Donald C. *The Rhetorical Uses of the Authorizing Figure: Fidel Castro and José Martí*. New York: Praeger, 1992.

Rigby, T. H. "Introduction: Political Legitimacy, Weber, and Communist Mono-organizational Systems." *Political Legitimation in Communist States*. T.H. Rigby and Ferenc Feher, ed. New York: St. Martin's Press, 1982.

Riskin, Carl. "Neither Plan nor Market: Mao's Political Economy." In *New Perspectives on the Cultural Revolution*, William A. Joseph, Christine P. W. Wong, and David Zweig, eds. Cambridge: Harvard University Press, 1991, 133–52.

Rosen, Stanley. "Students and the State in China: The Crisis in Ideology and Organization." In *State and Society in China: The Consequences of Reform*, Arthur Lewis Rosenbaum, ed. Boulder, Colo.: Westview Press, 1992, 167.

——— . "The Impact of Reform Policies on Youth Attitudes." In *Chinese Society on the Eve of Tiananmen*, D. Davis and E. F. Vogel, eds. Cambridge, Mass.: Harvard University Press, 1990: 283–305.

————. "The Effect of Post–June 4 Reeducation Campaigns on Chinese Students," *China Quarterly* 134, June 1993, 310–25.

Rushing, Janice Hocker. "The Rhetoric of the American Western Myth." *Communication Monographs* 50 (1983):14–32.

Safire, William. "Greatest Leap Forward." *New York Times*, 10 December 1984.

Sahliyeh, Emile. "Religious Resurgence and Political Modernization." In *Religious Resurgence and Politics in the Contemporary World*, Emile Sahliyeh, ed. Albany: State University of New York Press, 1990.

Salisbury, Harrison E. *The New Emperors: China in the Era of Mao and Deng*. Boston: Little, Brown, 1992.

Sangren, Steven. *History and Magical Power in a Chinese Community*. Stanford: Stanford University Press, 1987.

————. "History and the Rhetoric of Legitimacy: The Ma Tsu Cult of Taiwan," *Comparative Studies in Society and History* 30 (1988):674–97.

Schoenhals, Michael. *Doing Things with Words in Chinese Politics*. Berkeley: Institute of East Asian Studies, 1992.

Schram, Stuart. *Mao Zedong: A Preliminary Reassessment*. Hong Kong: Chinese University Press, 1983.

Schram, Stuart R. "'Economics in Command?' Ideology and Policy Since the Third Plenum, 1978–84." *China Quarterly* 99 (1984):419.

Schwartz, Benjamin I. *Communism and China: Ideology in Flux*. Cambridge, Mass.: Harvard University Press, 1968.

————. "The Reign of Virtue: Some Broad Perspectives on Leader and Party in the Cultural Revolution." In *Party Leadership and Revolutionary Power in China*, John Wilson Lewis, ed. Cambridge: Cambridge University Press, 1970.

Sharma, Ram Naresh. "Mao's Concepts of Power, Authority, and Legitimacy." *China Report* 25, 2 (1989):135–145.

Shue, Vivienne. *The Reach of the State*. Stanford: Stanford University Press, 1988.

Singh, Kusum J. "Gandhi and Mao as Mass Communicators." *Journal of Communication* (1976), 94–101.

Solomon, Martha. "The Positive Woman's Journey: A Mythic Analysis of the Rhetoric of Stop ERA." *Quarterly Journal of Speech* 65 (1979), 262–74.

Spence, Jonathan. *The Search for Modern China*. New York: W. W. Norton, 1990.

Starr, John Bryan. *Ideology and Culture*. New York: Harper and Row, 1973.

Teiwes, Frederick C. *Leadership, Legitimacy, and Conflict in China*. Armonk, N.Y.: M. E. Sharpe, 1984.

Thaxton, Ralph. *China Turned Rightside Up: Revolutionary Legitimacy in the Peasant World*. New Haven: Yale University Press, 1983.

The Thirteenth Party Congress and China's Reforms. Beijing: Beijing Review Press, 1987.

"Third Party Plenum Communique Discussed throughout Country," Foreign Broadcast Information Service-China, 28 December 1978:E1.

Uhalley, Jr., Stephen. *A History of the Chinese Communist Party*. Stanford: Hoover Institution Press, 1988.

Urban, George, ed. *The Miracles of Chairman Mao*. London: Tom Stacey, 1971.

Wakeman, Frederick "Revolutionary Rites: The Remains of Chiang Kai-shek and Mao Tse-tung." *Representations* 10 (1985):167–68.

Weber, Max. *Economy and Society: An Outline of Interpretive Sociology*. New York: Bedminster Press, 1968.

Weng, Byron S. J. "Introduction." In *Mao Zedong: A Preliminary Reassessment*, Stuart Schram, ed. Hong Kong: Chinese University Press, 1983.

Whyte, M. "The Social Sources of the Student Demonstrations." In *China Briefing, 1990*, A. J. Kane, ed. Boulder, Colo.: Westview Press, 1990, 47–63.

Wu An-chia. "The 'Initial Stage of Socialism': Background, Tasks, and Impact." In *Mainland China after the Thirteenth Party Congress*. King-yuh Chang, ed. Boulder, Colo.: Westview Press, 1990.

Yan Jiaqi. *Toward a Democratic China*. Honolulu: University of Hawaii Press, 1992.

Zhao Ziyang "Advance along the Road of Socialism with Chinese Characteristics," in *Documents of the Thirteenth National Congress of the Communist Party of China (1987)*. Beijing: Foreign Language Press, 1987.

Index